Writing Skills

McGraw-Hill Basic Skills

Tools for Learning Success

Dr. Alton L. Raygor, Consulting Editor

STUDY SKILLS	READING	VOCABULARY	SPELLING	WRITING	MATHEMATICS
Yates: *Listening and Note-Taking*	Fisher: *Reading to Discover Organization*	Davis: *Basic Vocabulary Skills*	LTI: *Basic Spelling Skills*	Shew and Pincar: *Writing Skills*	Eraut: *Fundamentals of Arithmetic*
LTI: *Library Skills*	Fisher: *Reading to Understand Science*				Eraut: *Fundamentals of Elementary Algebra*
Raygor and Wark: *Systems for Study*	Harnadak: *Critical Reading Improvement*				Eraut: *Fundamentals of Intermediate Algebra*
Samson: *Problem Solving Improvement*	Maxwell: *Skimming and Scanning Skills*				
Wark and Mogen: *Read, Underline, Review*	Raygor and Schick: *Reading at Efficient Rates*				
	Raygor: *Reading for the Main Idea*				
	Raygor: *Reading for Significant Facts*				

Pretests and Posttests are available to measure progress.

Editor's Introduction

This book is part of a system of materials—McGraw-Hill Basic Skills: Tools for Learning Success. Designed at the University of Minnesota Reading and Study Skills Center, Basic Skills is aimed at college-bound high school students, and junior college and college students who need to improve those skills necessary for academic success. The system consists of *tests* to determine instructional needs and *materials* designed to meet those needs, plus an instructor's manual to explain the tests and materials and the relationship between them. The purpose of the *tests* is to find out what instruction a student needs in basic skills; the purpose of the *materials* is to give that instruction. Each student gets what he or she needs, without wasting time on unnecessary tasks.

Six basic skill topics—study, reading, vocabulary, spelling, writing, and mathematics—are covered, and two tests (A and B forms) are provided for each topic. Subscales on the tests are matched to accompanying instructional materials: thus a student with a low score on one or more subscales gets instruction in the corresponding skill. The second form of the test may be used to evaluate progress after instruction.

The instructional materials are designed to be used separately, if desired, and can be purchased as single units. Most of the materials are suitable for adoption as textbooks in such basic skill courses as Freshman English, Communications, How to Study, Vocabulary Development, and Remedial or Developmental Mathematics. Individualized diagnosis and instruction are optional in such settings.

This second edition, prepared after several years of successful use of the first edition, provides several new features that will make it even more useful. The three books have been combined into one effective program. The material is extremely well organized to teach skills in the early parts that are used in the later parts.

The authors have done many things to increase the clarity, the diagnostic features, and the down-to-earth utility of the material, and they have done so in a pleasant, interesting style.

The main objectives of the authors were to focus on student life in college and to promote strategies for effective study. The authors have done both, and have produced an extremely effective instructional tool.

Alton L. Raygor
Consulting Editor
University of Minnesota

Writing Skills

A Program for Self-Instruction

SECOND EDITION

PHILLIP SHEW
Nova University

DEBRA PINCAR
California State University
Fullerton

McGRAW-HILL BOOK COMPANY
New York St. Louis San Francisco Auckland Bogotá Düsseldorf
Johannesburg London Madrid Mexico Montreal New Delhi
Panama Paris São Paulo Singapore Sydney Tokyo Toronto

Writing Skills

1 2 3 4 5 6 7 8 9 0 DODO 7 8 3 2 1 0 9

This book was set in Paladium by Allen Wayne Technical Corp.
The editor was William A. Talkington and the production supervisor was Donna Piligra.
R. R. Donnelley & Sons Company was printer and binder.

Library of Congress Cataloging in Publication Data

Shew, Phillip.
Writing skills.

"McGraw-Hill basic skills."
1. English language—Rhetoric. 2. English language—Composition and exercises. 3. English language—Grammar—1950- I. Pincar, Debra, joint author. II. Title.
PE1417.S43 1980 808'.042 79-14066
ISBN 0-07-056690-9

Contents

To the Instructor

This book attempts to set forth a clear system for enabling college students to express their intended meaning effectively in both sentences and paragraphs—the basic necessities for good writing.

The revision of three prior texts into one has combined the original traditional grammar emphasis with one that is rooted in transformational grammar and rhetoric. The existing structural strengths of the original text have been maintained, with editing aimed at conciseness and student involvement.

It is hoped that the student will develop a personally useful set of strategies and rules for writing from the ideas presented in this text. The stories and examples were based on two major criteria: student life in college and strategies for effective study.

It is possible to measure growth in knowledge of writing rules by using the companion McGraw-Hill Writing Test. For best use of the text in relation to the test, start with the diagnostic item analysis of the student's writing strengths and weaknesses. Through using specific parts of the text and periodic criterion reference check tests to strengthen diagnosed areas of weakness, the student should be able to progress toward proficiency as a college-level writer.

In order to have the option of directly measuring growth in writing fluency, we are also including a writing sample evaluation form on page **xii**. Such a form can be modified to your individual tests. The idea is to be able to evaluate systematically the student's actual writing and to be able to get pre- and posttest indices of the student's progress in writing. It may very well be a good idea to generally review for the student a system for organizing his or her initial writing sample theme. The following approach has proved helpful in getting our developmental students started: (1) Identify a topic to write about (you may wish to provide that for the student); (2) brainstorm all the ideas the student can think of on the topic; (3) eliminate all ideas that are not important to the topic as delimited; (4) group related ideas together; and (5) arrange the groups in the order that the writer feels makes most sense. Such a system will enable the student to start out in theme writing. *Writing Skills* should improve the sentence and paragraph skills necessary for writing a polished theme.

Acknowledgments

There are many people who have contributed to this text. The Jersey City State College students who have offered suggestions were most helpful. Ellen Fuchs, Don Burden, and Bill Talkington, our editors from McGraw-Hill, offered initial inspiration, sound advice, and warm encouragement. Bob Bently of Lansing Community College, Pat Hartwell of the University of Cincinnati, and Jane Eeder of Manhattan Community College shaped much of the direction of this revised edition with their penetrating reviews. Mark Edmonds and Greg Waters of the University of Michigan, Flint; John Langan of Atlantic Community College; Dave Zwengler of Rutgers University College; Ed Ezor, Liliane MacPherson, and Ted Lane of Jersey City State College provided reinforcement through their shared similar beliefs about the way writing should be taught. Gary Spencer, Jim Hengoed, Hans Held, and Bob Latzer of Jersey City State College have been tremendously supportive allies as administrators of the programs in which we've taught. Thanks most especially to Bobby Kargenian and Candace Freeman for doing the typing and the copying and for offering valuable suggestions about content despite the rigors of their own schedule as full-time students.

Phillip Shew
Debra Pincar

To the Student

Writing skill can be helpful in a variety of situations. Many times we write, only to find that our message was misunderstood by our reader. For instance, students often do poorly on essay tests, not because they don't know the answers, but because they cannot explain their thoughts on paper. Many graduates miss out on job interviews because they cannot write personal letters to prospective employers. Furthermore, people are often held back from job opportunities or promotions because of their limited writing skill.

Good writing begins with understanding how to construct and use effective sentences and paragraphs. The intent of this book is to enable you to acquire skill in writing sentences and paragraphs that will be useful to you in a wide variety of situations.

In this book we will set up questions and examples for you, and you will write your answers directly in the book. You can check your answers as you go along. This approach is designed to help you become your own instructor, editor, and critic, so that your writing expresses your intention to your readers. To see how you do this, turn now to the next page.

Phillip Shew
Debra Pincar

Writing Sample

Student's Name: ______________________

Social Security Number: ______________________

Reader's Name: ______________________

Number of Words in the Writing Sample: __________

PROBLEM	NUMBER OF ERRORS	NUMBER OF ERRORS PER 50 WORDS
1. Sentence fragments	______	______
2. Subject-verb agreement	______	______
3. Verb tenses	______	______
4. Compound sentences: use of commas and connectives	______	______
5. Run-on sentences and comma splices	______	______
6. Complex sentences and their punctuation, including the semicolon	______	______
7. Commas to set off introductory and parenthetical elements	______	______
8. Commas and semicolons in a series	______	______
9. Faulty parallelism	______	______
10. Dangling modifiers	______	______
11. Mixed constructions	______	______
12. Shifts in number, tense, and person	______	______
13. Pronoun forms	______	______
14. Faulty pronoun reference	______	______
15. Modifier forms	______	______
16. Spelling	______	______
17. Omitted words	______	______
18. Terminal punctuation	______	______

Section 1
The Sentence

In this section, we will give you some clues for writing good sentences. We will begin working with simple sentences and then proceed to more difficult ones. As you write frequently and compare what you write with what you read, you will develop your own guidelines for writing.

When you finish this chapter you will be able to (1) identify sentences and clauses; (2) avoid the two most common sentence mistakes, the fragment and run-on; and (3) differentiate among the three basic sentence types—simple, compound, and complex.

This program will not try to teach every English rule. Instead, we will help you get in touch with the logical connections that can be made between the natural oral language which you've already learned and the written language which you are learning.

The basic idea in writing is the same as it is in speaking. The sender of a message is trying to transfer his intended meaning to a receiver. People can communicate the same message in many ways. For example, when a baby falls down, he cries. When an older child falls down, she might say, "ow!" An adult who falls down might say, "My knee hurts!"

1

In writing, the form for expressing a message or idea is called the sentence. A sentence expresses a complete idea. It names who or what we are talking about, and it tells us something about it. Which of the examples above is communicating by means of a sentence?

The adult is using a sentence.

2

Look at this sentence: He yawns.

1. Which word answers the question, Who yawns?

   ____

2. Which word answers the question, He does what?

   ____

1. He (it names who we are talking about)
2. yawns (tells us something about him)

3

Now read these sentences. Then answer the questions that illustrate how a sentence explains itself.

1. Babies cry.
   a. Who cries?

   ____

   b. Babies do what?

   ____

2. George smokes.
   a. Who smokes?

   ____

   b. George does what?

   ____

1. *a.* Babies
   b. cry
2. *a.* George
   b. smokes

4

You can conclude that a sentence must contain at least (Check the correct answer.)

______ *a.* one basic part
______ *b.* two basic parts
______ *c.* three basic parts

b

5

There are names for the two basic parts of a sentence. You have probably heard these names before—subject and verb.

In "He yawns," the *subject* is the word that answers the question, Who yawns?

In the blank below, write the subject of the sentence "He yawns."

____

He

6

The verb is the word that answers the question, He does what?

In the sentence "He yawns," what is the verb?

____

yawns

7

Read this sentence: Lightning strikes.

1. *a.* What strikes?

   ____

   b. The *subject* of this sentence is ______________________________.

2. *a.* Lightning does what?

   ____

   b. The *verb* of this sentence is ______________________________.

1. *a.* Lightning
   b. Lightning
2. *a.* strikes
   b. strikes

8

Two-word sentences are the *simplest* types of sentence. In two-word sentences, one word must be the ______________ and the other the ______________.

(Either order)
subject
verb

9

From your answer to the last frame, you can see that all sentences *must* have a ______________ and a ______________.

(Either order)
subject
verb

You may be thinking that people can and do communicate clearly without using sentences. For example, if someone asks, "Who went with you?" and your answer is "George," you will be understood.

However, when you speak, you have an advantage that you don't have when you write—if someone doesn't understand what you say to her, she can ask you what you mean. If she doesn't understand something you have written, you may not be around to explain it.

10

People will understand what you write much better if you ____________ use complete sentences. (do) (do not)

do

Every sentence has a subject and verb—but not all groups of words with a subject and verb are sentences. A sentence should express a complete idea. It should make sense. Look at this group of words: "He went to." This group of words has a subject ("He") and a verb ("went"). Is it a sentence?

____

no

11

"The noisy crowd" is not a sentence because it doesn't express a complete idea. It makes you ask questions like: What about the noisy crowd? Are these two groups of words sentences?

1. The disco was crowded.
   Answer ____________
   (yes) (no)

2. The crowded disco.
   Answer ____________
   (yes) (no)

1. yes
2. no

12

"The crowded disco" does not express a complete thought. It leaves the reader wondering "What happened at the crowded disco?" More information is needed in order for this sentence to make sense. Tell what happened at the crowded disco. For example:

Intimacy was difficult at the crowded disco.

or

The crowded disco excites me.

Writing good sentences becomes easier if you remember these three clues. Ask yourself:

1. Is there a subject?
2. Is there a verb?
3. Does what I'm saying make sense?

Are these groups of words sentences? If not, add what is missing and make them into sentences. Have your instructor check your work.

1 He ate.
(Answer yes or no) ______________________________

____

____

2. After he ate.
(Answer yes or no) ______________________________

____

____

3. While it rained.
(Answer yes or no) ______________________________

____

____

4. Before the concert.
(Answer yes or no) ______________________________

____

____

1. yes
2. No, add what happened after he ate.
3. No, add what happened while it rained.
4. No, add what happened before the concert.

13

There are three clues to writing good sentences. Let's review them. Write them in the blanks provided.

____

____

____

1. A sentence has a subject.
2. A sentence has a verb.
3. A sentence expresses a complete idea. It makes sense.

14

Now that we can write sentences, we can make our writing more interesting by adding more information to them. Let's go back to the sentence "He ate." We know that it is a sentence because it has a subject, a verb, and it makes sense. However, if more information were added we would know more about what he ate. For example:

He ate the sandwich.

Sandwich explains what he ate.

The term for the words used to complete the thought by telling who or what is *object*. In the sentence above, "sandwich" is the object. Pick out the object in the following sentences. Remember the two clues for finding the object: it answers the question who or what the subject did.

1. He fixed the car.
2. The secretary answered the telephone.

1. car
2. telephone

15

So far, you have been working with sentences that contain one idea. Such a sentence is called a *simple sentence.*

Let's see what happens when you connect two simple sentences, using the connecting word "and." Write your answer in the blank provided.

I turned the corner. (and) I saw him.

____

I turned the corner and I saw him.

(Notice that the two simple sentences are related to each other.)

16

The sentence you have just written is called a *compound sentence.* The difference between a compound sentence and a simple sentence is that a simple sentence expresses one idea and the compound sentence expresses ______ (how many?) related ideas.

two (or more)

17

What type of sentence is each of these sentences?

1. They loaned him a car.
   Answer ______________
   (simple) (compound)
2. It was out of gas.
   Answer ______________
   (simple) (compound)
3. They loaned him a car, and it was out of gas.
   Answer ______________
   (simple) (compound)

1. simple
2. simple
3. compound

18

So far, the examples of compound sentences you have seen used "and" as a connecting word. The words "but" and "or" are also used as connecting words in compound sentences.

Combine the following simple sentences to make compound sentences, using "but" or "or" as a connecting word (whichever makes sense).

1. I wrote to him. He didn't answer.

   ____

2. All dogs are animals. Not all animals are dogs.

   ____

3. Was the instructor really sick? Did she go skiing?

   ____

1. I wrote to him, but he didn't answer.
2. All dogs are animals, but not all animals are dogs.
3. Was the instructor really sick, or did she go skiing?

You probably noticed that in our answers to frame 18 we put *commas* before the connecting words. Usually it is necessary to punctuate compound sentences this way (unless the sentence is very short). In all our answers, we will punctuate complete sentences as they should be punctuated. You should *notice* where the commas are, but don't worry about getting them exactly right in all the sentences *you* are writing now. Later on in this text you will do a section entirely on punctuation. In that section you will practice using commas correctly in your own sentences.

19

You've probably heard the word *clause* before—more times than you would have liked. Let's see how clauses work in a compound sentence.

Once two simple sentences are joined by "and," "but," or "or" to form a compound sentence, they are called clauses.

What are the two clauses in the sentence "I turned the corner and I saw him"?

____

____

I turned the corner
I saw him

20

Now look again at these sentences:

I wrote to him, but he didn't answer.
All dogs are animals, but not all animals are dogs.
Was the instructor really sick, or did she go skiing?

How many clauses does *each* of these sentences have?

____

two

21

Which of the following sentences has *two* clauses? (*Check the correct answer.*)

_______ *a.* We drove the small car.
_______ *b.* They followed us in the van.
_______ *c.* We drove the small car, and they followed us in the van.

c

22

Look again at this sentence:

We drove the small car, and they followed us in the van.

1. The first clause is:

   ____

2. The second clause is:

   ____

1. We drove the small car
2. they followed us in the van

23

Does each clause in the sentence "We drove the small car, and they followed us in the van" have a *subject* and *verb*?

Answer ____________
(yes) (no)

yes

24
A clause *always* has a subject and a verb.

Which of the following is a *clause*?

a. chases Volkswagens
b. the dog chases Volkswagens

Answer ______________
(*a*) or (*b*)

b

25
A compound sentence contains at least ______________ clauses.

two

26
Now read the following *simple* sentence carefully:

He followed my advice and lost the game.

1. How many *subjects* are there in the sentence?

____

2. How many *verbs* are there?

____

3. Does the sentence contain one clause or two clauses?

____

1. one
2. two
3. one clause

(The word group "lost the game" contains no subject, and a clause must have *both* a subject and a verb.)

27

If a sentence contains two verbs and only one subject, both verbs must apply to the same subject—like this:

He followed my advice and (he) lost the game.

Now look at this sentence:

She saw the tow truck and moved her car.

In the blank below, fill in the word that shows how the two verbs apply to the same subject.

She saw the tow truck and (________________) moved her car.

She saw the tow truck and (*she*) moved her car.

28

Compare these two sentences:

a. She saw the tow truck and moved her car.
b. She saw the tow truck, and she moved her car.

Which sentence is composed of two *clauses* joined by a *connecting word?*

Answer ____________
(*a*) or (*b*)

b

29

To see why sentence *a* does *not* have two clauses, try dividing it into different sections. For example:

She saw the tow truck   and moved her car.
She saw the tow truck and   moved her car.

Can you find a way to divide the above sentence into two parts so that *each* part has a subject and a verb?

____

It's impossible, isn't it?

30

Sentence *a* ("She saw the tow truck and moved her car.") and sentence *b* (She saw the tow truck, and she moved her car.") are two different types of sentences.

1. Sentence *a cannot* be divided into two parts so that each part has a subject and a verb. Therefore, sentence *a* is a ____________________ sentence.
2. Sentence *b can* be divided into two parts so that each part has a subject and a verb. (Also, the two parts are joined by "and.") Therefore, sentence *b* is a ____________________ sentence.

1. simple
2. compound

31

Our writing can become more interesting if we join simple sentences into compound sentences. The following paragraph gives clues and examples of how this can be done. Read the paragraph over, and notice the sentence structure. Then, using what you have just learned, rewrite the paragraph, following the directions below it. (Some of the sentences we rewrite will be simple sentences; some will be compound.)

a. Let's consider the subject "Women's Changing Role in Society."
b. I will describe the world of women.
c. I will describe their traditional duties.
d. We will see new opportunities becoming available to women.
e. We will analyze the problems they encounter.
f. Women today are beginning to be independent, but women today must overcome many obstacles.
g. Their traditional duty is marriage, this means being confined to the home.

Directions:

1. Combine sentences *b* and *c* to make *one* sentence, using the connecting word "and." Omit the words "I will describe" from the second sentence.

____

____

2. Combine *d* and *e* to make *one* complete sentence.

____

____

3. In sentence *f*, "women today" is repeated in each clause. Drop "women today" from the second clause.

4. In sentence *g*, connect the two clauses with the connecting word "and."

1. I will describe the world of women, and their traditional duties.
2. We will see new opportunities becoming available to women, and we will analyze the problems they encounter.
3. Women today are beginning to be independent, but must overcome many obstacles.
4. Their traditional duty is marriage, and this means being confined to the home.

32

Beginning with sentence *a* in the previous frame, write out the entire paragraph using the new sentence structure you just formed.

Let's consider the subject "Women's Changing Role in Society." I will describe the world of women, and their traditional duties. We will see new opportunities becoming available to women, and we will see the problems they encounter. Women today are beginning to be independent, but must overcome many obstacles. Their traditional duty is marriage, and this means being confined to the home.

33

Direction 1 in frame 31 told you to combine sentences *b* and *c*:

b. I will describe the world of women.
c. I will describe their traditional duties.

Read these two sentences aloud. In sentence *c*, when you say "their problems," you know that you mean "women's problems." Where did you learn this?

____

from sentence *b*

34

In frame 31, there is a word in sentence *c*—"their"—that you can only understand by looking at sentence *b*. Sentence *c* further explains sentence *b*. When two ideas are related, we can join them into one sentence. You can see also that each sentence begins with "I will describe." Because two ideas are closely related, and we know the same person is talking, we can omit the second "I will describe." You can just as easily understand the meaning of the sentence without being told again who is describing. The new sentence will both sound better and show the relationship between the two ideas more clearly.

By combining sentences *b* and *c* with the connecting word "and," and by omitting the words "I will describe," you created a ______________ (simple) (compound) sentence.

Simple—you dropped the subject and verb from the second clause. We now have a simple sentence with only one subject and one verb.

35

Look back at sentence *a* in frame 31 for a moment. Let's consider the subject "Women's Changing Role in Society." Sentence *a* is a *topic sentence*—a sentence that tells you what the paragraph is going to be about. You probably noticed that we didn't combine this sentence with any other one. This was because it is *correct* and because a short topic sentence will usually make it easier for a reader to understand what your paragraph is about.

36

Direction 2 in frame 31 told you to combine *d* and *e* with the word "and."

d. We will see the new opportunities becoming available to women.
e. We will see the problems they encounter.

By connecting these two sentences, we've created a ________________ sentence.

compound

37

Direction 3 in frame 31 told you to drop the *second* "women today" from sentence *f*:

f. Women today are beginning to be independent, but women today must overcome many obstacles.

If you read the above sentence aloud, you can tell that the second "women today" is unnecessary. You can just as easily understand *who* must overcome many obstacles without being told the subject again. By dropping the second "women today," you are making this ________________ sentence a ________________ sentence, because you are dropping the ________________ of the second clause.

compound
simple
subject

38

Direction 4 told you to *connect* the two clauses with the word "and."

g. Their traditional duty is marriage,
this means being confined to the home.

By combining these two clauses we are making a ________________ sentence.

compound

39

The next paragraph is similar in structure to the paragraph given in frame 31. Rewrite the following paragraph to improve it in the same way you did in the preceding paragraph. Again, the first sentence is a topic sentence and needs no rewriting.

> In ancient Egypt women enjoyed favorable conditions. The couple was the social unit. Women were equal to men. Women acquired fortunes. As large as many men's. Also, they inherited property and they exercised power. A woman married without compulsion. She could marry again if widowed.

____

____

____

____

____

____

____

____

In ancient Egypt women enjoyed favorable conditions. The couple was the social unit, and women were equal to men. Women acquired fortunes as large as many men's. Also, they inherited property and exercised power. A woman married without compulsion, and she could marry again if widowed.

You can see from comparing the original paragraph with the rewritten one that knowing how different types of sentences are formed can help you write better. You can be a clearer, more effective writer if you check your own work for similar ways to improve your writing.

40

Rewrite the following paragraph to improve it in the same way you did in the preceding paragraph. When you finish, first check your own work, then review what you've done with your instructor.

> Dieting is definitely not my idea of fun. A week of nothing but cottage cheese is making my life miserable! A week of nothing but Tab is making my life miserable! My sleep is haunted by nightmares of tempting banana splits. Piled high with mounds of whipped cream and hot fudge topping. Potato chips seem to come alive and dare me to eat just one.
>
> I toss and turn in bed for hours, trying to resist temptation, and a McDonald's jingle begins to run through my head.
>
> "I'll go crazy if this keeps up," I mutter to myself. So rather than ending up in an insane asylum, I glance over at my husband to make sure he's still asleep. I reach over to the dresser. I quietly open the top drawer. Before its creaking can ever be heard, I pop a Hershey kiss into my mouth, roll over, and settle down for a good night's sleep.

Dieting is definitely not my idea of fun. A week of nothing but cottage cheese and Tab is making my life miserable! My sleep is haunted by nightmares of banana splits, piled high with mounds of whipped cream and hot fudge topping. Potato chips seem to come alive and dare me to eat just one.

I toss and turn in bed for hours, trying to resist temptation, and a McDonald's jingle begins to run through my head.

"I'll go crazy if this keeps up," I mutter to myself. So rather than ending up in an insane asylum, I glance over at my husband to make sure he's still asleep, reach over to the dresser, and quietly open the top drawer. Before its creaking can ever be heard, I pop a Hershey kiss into my mouth, roll over, and settle down for a good night's sleep.

41

You have learned several things to check for in the sentences you write. For example, look at this group of words: "All of a sudden."

1. Is this group of words a sentence? ____________
(yes) (no)

2. Explain your answer. ____________________________________

____

____

1. no
(*Your own words*)
2. It has neither a *subject* nor a *verb*. It doesn't express a complete idea.

42

When you write, you must check to be sure every sentence you write has a subject and verb. Also, be on the lookout for words like "if," "when," "unless," "because," "after," "since," and "until."

1. Is this a sentence?
I heard about them.

____

2. Is this a sentence?
After I heard about them.

____

1. yes
2. no

43

"After I heard about them" is not a sentence because it isn't a complete thought. It raises questions it doesn't answer, such as: "What happened after I heard about them?"

Which word in "After I heard about them" causes the problem?

____

after

44

Suppose you are checking a paper you have written. You spot this group of words: "If my conclusion is true."

You are not sure whether "If my conclusion is true" is a sentence. You ask youself, Does it have a subject and a verb? The answer is ________________.

yes

45

"If my conclusion is true" has both a subject and a verb, but that alone does not make it a sentence.

Suppose someone said to you, "If my conclusion is true." Would you know what he was talking about?

Answer ____________
(yes) (no)

no

46

"If my conclusion is true" does not express a complete idea. It raises questions like: What happens if my conclusion is true? Therefore, it ____________ a sentence.
(is) (is not)

is not

47

Suppose, in your paper, the sentence directly following "If my conclusion is true" is this: "The Income Tax Bureau is in trouble."

Does this answer the question of what happens if my conclusion is true?

____

yes

48

Combine "If my conclusion is true" and "The Income Tax Bureau is in trouble" so that they form a sentence.

____

____

If my conclusion is true, the Income Tax Bureau is in trouble.

49

Look at these two groups of words as they originally appeared in your term paper:

a. The Income Tax Bureau is in trouble.
b. If my conclusion is true.

1. Are (*a*) and (*b*) clauses?

   Answer ____________
   (yes) (no)

2. Explain your answer. ______________________________

   ____

1. yes
2. Both (*a*) and (*b*) have subjects and verbs.

50

One of the two clauses in the previous frame could stand alone as a complete sentence. Which of the two clauses—"The Income Tax Bureau is in trouble" or "If my conclusion is true"—is also a complete sentence?

____

"The Income Tax Bureau is in trouble."

51

A clause that can stand alone as a complete sentence is a different type of clause from one that cannot.

The names for these two types of clauses are *independent* and *dependent.*

Look again at the two clauses:

a. The Income Tax Bureau is in trouble.
b. If my conclusion is true.

1. Which of these clauses is independent?

   Answer ____________
   (*a*) or (*b*)

2. Which of these clauses is dependent?

Answer ____________
(*a*) or (*b*)

1. *a*
2. *b*

52

A dependent clause ________________ stand alone, while an independent
(can) (cannot)
clause ________________ stand alone.
(can) (cannot)

cannot
can

53

Now look at these two sentences:

a. When I write, I'll send my new address.
b. I'll write to you and I'll send my new address.

1. Which sentence has one *independent* clause and one *dependent* clause?

Answer ____________
(*a*) or (*b*)

2. Which sentence has two independent clauses?

Answer ____________
(*a*) or (*b*)

1. *a*
2. *b*

54

Write out the *dependent* clause in the sentence, "When I write, I'll send my new address."

____

When I write

55

The following sentences contain one dependent clause and one independent clause. *Write out* the *independent* clauses on the line provided.

1. If I see her, I'll tell her about the call.

   ____

2. Because they were worried, we went back early.

   ____

3. When the president spoke, the audience became quiet.

   ____

4. They didn't leave until they were forced to.

   ____

5. Several people walked out when they heard the news.

   ____

1. I'll tell her about the call
2. we went back early
3. the audience became quiet
4. They didn't leave
5. Several people walked out

56

In column A below are *independent* clauses. In column B below are *dependent* clauses. Put the two columns together to form new complete sentences, and write these sentences in the blanks provided.

A	B
you spoke to her	when she argued with you

1. ______________________________

A	B
the test was handed out	before anybody could leave

2. ______________________________

A	B
they blamed the owner	because repairs weren't made

3. ______________________________

1. You spoke to her when she argued with you. *or*
   When she argued with you, you spoke to her.
2. The test was handed out before anybody could leave. *or*
   Before anybody could leave, the test was handed out.
3. They blamed the owner because repairs weren't made. *or*
   Because repairs weren't made, they blamed the owner.

57

The sentences you just wrote are called *complex* sentences.

Complex sentences: (*Check the correct answer.*)

______ *a.* cannot be divided into two separate clauses
______ *b.* consist of two independent clauses joined by "and," "but," or "or"
______ *c.* consist of one independent clause and at least one dependent clause

c

(If you checked answer *a*, go back and review frame 30. If you checked answer *b*, go back and review frame 19. When you've done this, return to frame 58 and continue.)

58

When words like "when," "if," "because," "before," "after," "since," and "until" introduce a clause, the clause becomes dependent on the rest of the sentence.

To see how this works, look at this sentence in which the dependent clause is italicized:

She was angry *when I got home.*

1. Write out the clause that tells what happened "when I got home."

   ____

2. This clause is (a, an) ______________________ clause.
   (dependent) (independent)

1. She was angry
2. independent

59

The dependent clause is called "dependent" because it can't stand alone as a sentence and because its meaning depends upon the ________________ clause.

independent

60

Look at the following examples:

before the revolution
before the revolution started

Which of the following is a dependent clause?

a. before the revolution
b. before the revolution started
c. both of the above

Answer ____________
(*a*), (*b*), (*c*)

b
Only (*b*) is a clause—because it has a subject and a verb.

61

"Before the revolution" is not a sentence. It is dependent upon other words in order to mean something. For example:

The general fled before the revolution.

However, "before the revolution" is not a dependent clause. Explain why.

____

____

(*Your own words*)
"Before the revolution" does not have a subject and verb.
(*Note that if there is not a subject and a verb present, there cannot be a sentence or a clause.*)

62

Some of the following groups of words are dependent clauses and some are not. In those that are dependent clauses, underline the subject once and underline the verb twice.

a. before the sound of the gun

b. after the war was over

c. until the thirtieth of December

d. since I last saw her

e. if that poverty-stricken old man

b. war was

d. I saw

63

Remember that a *complex* sentence has one independent clause and at least one dependent clause.

Some of the following sentences are *simple* sentences and some are *complex.* For each of the *complex* sentences, underline the *dependent* clause.

a. Since the game is over, we've lost.
b. You shouldn't tell her anything when she asks.
c. Before she moved away, their relationship was different.
d. Before the opening of the play, the roof fell in.
e. We can't do anything until daylight.

a. Since the game is over
b. when she asks
c. Before she moved away

64

In complex sentences, a definite relationship exists between ideas in the independent and dependent clauses. Being aware of this can help you solve one of the most common writing problems that students have: mistaking dependent clauses for sentences.

Read the next paragraph to see if you can spot the nonsentences. Then *rewrite* the paragraph, using what you know about complex sentences to correct the mistakes.

> We can remember people's tears. When Marilyn Monroe died. Movie stars are worshipped. Because their worshippers' lives are unsatisfactory. Hero worship is an "ideal" relationship. If the *real* relationships in a person's life are empty. He will then have imaginary relationships with unreal heroes.

____

____

____

____

____

____

____

____

We can remember people's tears when Marilyn Monroe died. Movie stars are worshipped because their worshippers' lives are unsatisfactory. Hero worship is an "ideal" relationship. If the *real* relationships in a person's life are empty, he will then have imaginary relationships with unreal heroes.

65

The nonsentences in this paragraph were all *dependent clauses* that were closely related to the sentences. For this reason, you combined them with the sentences to form new ____________________ sentences.

(complex) (simple)

complex

66

In the following paragraph, the mistakes are the same as in the previous example: dependent clauses are used as sentences. Correct them just as you did in the last example.

A housewife can become isolated. When she is alone all day with "things." A dish is gone forever. If it is broken. Every accident becomes a disaster. A housewife's security is shaky. As long as it depends on possessions rather than people.

A housewife can become isolated when she is alone all day with "things." A dish is gone forever if it is broken. Every accident becomes a disaster. A housewife's security is shaky as long as it depends on possessions rather than people.

67

Using the words "as long as" to introduce the dependent clause in the last sentence is probably new to you. In this example and in many others, "as long as" has the same effect as words like "if," "since," and "when."

In the paragraph you have just worked on, you learned to use your knowledge of complex sentences to avoid a common writing mistake: the *sentence fragment.* Sentence fragments (or nonsentences) are dependent clauses; they aren't sentences because they don't express a complete idea. If you had trouble correcting the paragraph, review frames 40 to 63. Now let's see how this knowledge can help you solve a different problem: using compound sentences when a complex sentence would express your ideas more clearly.

What is the difference between a *compound* and a *complex* sentence? We could answer this question by giving the definition of each, but that's not what we are after. We are concerned with how the two types of sentences differ in *written communication.*

Look at these two clauses:

he was sleepy
the job was boring

Which of the following sentences explains clearly why he was sleepy?

a. He was sleepy *and* the job was boring.
b. He was sleepy *because* the job was boring.

Answer ____________
(*a*) or (*b*)

b

68
The clauses "he was sleepy" and "the job was boring" sound peculiar when joined by "and" because it is not clear how the two ideas relate to each other. Take this example:

I will fly to Brazil *and* the weather in New York is clear.

Decide whether the above is a good compound sentence or a poor one, and then *explain* your decision in the space below.

____

____

____

If you decided that the compound sentence is a poor one because you can't tell how the two ideas relate to each other, we agree with you.

69
See if you can write a better version of "I will fly to Brazil *and* the weather in New York is clear" by using a connective word to form a complex sentence.

____

____

I will fly to Brazil *if* the weather in New York is clear.

70
The point we have been making in the last three frames cannot be a hard-and-fast rule. It is a matter of whether a sentence makes sense to the people who read it.

Read through the following compound sentences and label each one as *good* or *poor,* depending on how clearly the relationship between the ideas is expressed. Then check the answer to see if you agree with us.

1. ________________ I bought a novel, and I'm going to start it tonight.
2. ________________ I will finish the book tonight, and I am staying home.
3. ________________ We will ski tomorrow, and it snows tonight.
4. ________________ I laughed, and Sneed Hearn is a funny name.
5. ________________ Sneed Hearn accepted me into his group, and that made me very happy.

1. good
2. poor
3. poor
4. poor
5. good

71

Improve the three poor *compound* sentences, (sentences 2, 3, and 4) in the previous frame by making them into *complex* sentences. Instead of "and" use whichever connective words make sense.

2. ____

____

3. ____

____

4. ____

____

2. I will finish the book tonight because I am staying home.
3. We will ski tomorrow if it snows tonight.
4. I laughed because Sneed Hearn is a funny name.

72

Read through the following paragraph and locate any compound sentences that are unclear about how the two ideas (clauses) relate to each other. (*Hint: Watch out for the word "and."*)

Then rewrite the paragraph, changing the faulty compound sentences to complex sentences that clear up the clause relationship.

> Our class went to the museum Tuesday, and our design teacher wanted us to see the furniture exhibit. Most of the pieces displayed were very modern. One chair looked more like a car than a chair, and it was made of tubes of chrome. I sat down on it. I wouldn't want to own it, and it felt as uncomfortable as it looked.

____

____

____

____

____

____

____

____

Our class went to the museum Tuesday *because* our design teacher wanted us to see the furniture exhibit. Most of the pieces displayed were very modern. One chair looked more like a car than a chair *because* (or since) it was made of tubes of chrome. I sat down on it. I wouldn't want to own it, *because* it felt as uncomfortable as it looked.

73

Another way of improving writing is to be alert to common errors. Run-on sentences, along with sentence fragments, are the most frequently occurring sentence skills mistakes. Sentence fragments have already been covered in this chapter, because they are often confused with simple sentences. On the other hand, run-on sentences most often are confused with the two other kinds of sentences, compound and complex. A run-on sentence basically is two complete thoughts that are run together with no adequate punctuation provided to mark the break between them. Two hints are helpful before attempting to identify run-ons: 1) Read the passages aloud; try to hear where the major break in thought occurs. 2) Run-ons often occur when the second complete thought begins with one of the following words: I, you, he, she, it, we, they, there, this, that, then, next, now. There are three basic ways to correct a run-on sentence. The best method of correction depends on the kind of run-on error. If the thoughts are not closely related or if another kind of correction would make the sentence too long, use a period and a capital letter.

The following run-ons are the type which would be best corrected by using a period and a capital letter. Write your corrections on the blank below each run-on.

74
He never tries hard he's afraid of trying and failing.

He never tries hard. He's afraid of trying and failing.

75
She was embarrassed because she didn't drink I told her it didn't matter.

She was embarrassed because she didn't drink. I told her it didn't matter.

76
He had no way of stopping her from leaving that was something he couldn't help.

He had no way of stopping her from leaving. That was something he couldn't help.

77
He didn't know what to major in he liked too many subjects.

He didn't know what to major in. He liked too many subjects.

78
She tried to start the car repeatedly she thought the engine was just cold.

She tried to start the car repeatedly. She thought the engine was just cold.

The second and third kinds of run-on correction both involve two separate but closely related thoughts. In this instance, at the break between the thoughts, use a comma plus a joining word (e.g., and, but, for, so, or, nor, yet) to fuse the thoughts into one idea. It is also possible to obtain the same effect (if a joining word seems unnecessary) by using a semicolon.

Write your corrections on the blanks below each run-on.

79
He was dead tired he decided to go to bed before completing his assignment.

___

He was dead tired. He decided to go to bed before completing his assignment.

80
Men today have become more conscious of personal grooming they use cosmetics to better advantage than was formerly the case.

___

___

Men today have become more conscious of personal grooming, and they use cosmetics to better advantage than was formerly the case.

81
She had an upset stomach he gave her an antacid tablet.

___

She had an upset stomach, so he gave her an antacid tablet.

82
Carol washed her car in the morning it was dirty by afternoon.

___

Carol washed her car in the morning, but it was dirty by afternoon.

83

She had trouble doing her homework she told her boyfriend to stop distracting her.

She had trouble doing her homework; she told her boyfriend to stop distracting her.

These two types of run-ons, as well as the other elements presented in this section will be reviewed at later stages in this text. Now that you have an awareness of how sentences are formed and what the variations are, we are next going to look at punctuation as an aid to conveying our ideas in words to our readers.

Section 2 Punctuation and Capitalization

Punctuation

You have learned how to write simple, compound, and complex sentences. Now you'll learn how to punctuate them.

Punctuation basically compensates for the fact that the writer is not physically present to deliver a message to the reader. Thus, the writer has no way of giving the reader the normal cues used in speech to help clarify and emphasize the message. The tone and pitch of voice, pauses in speech, gestures, postures, facial expressions, touch, and so on all help the speaker to communicate with an audience. Punctuation serves this same purpose for us when we write. In this section we will give you some hints as to how the use of punctuation can make your writing easier to read.

Perhaps the most logical place to start is with those marks of punctuation which indicate that the writer has just expressed a complete thought. As we found out in the last section, the term used for expressing a complete thought is the *sentence.* When you finish this section, you will be able to punctuate your sentences so that it is clear whether they are statements, questions, or exclamations. You will be able to use commas in compound and complex sentences. You will also learn how to use capitalization in this section.

84

We've seen that there are many ways to express meaning in a sentence. Most of a sentence's meaning, of course, is expressed by the words—but there are parts of a sentence that are *not* words and can still help to express meaning. These are the *punctuation marks.*

Circle the punctuation marks in the following sentences:

I told him to drive.
I told him to drive!
Did I tell him to drive?

(.)
(!)
(?)

85

The punctuation marks you have just circled appear at the end of sentences and refer back to the *whole* sentence.

Look at the first sentence. The period (.) informs you that the sentence has ended and that it makes a *statement.*

Now look at the second sentence. The exclamation mark (!) informs you that the sentence has ended, but it also tells you that the sentence is not just a statement but an *exclamation.*

The difference in *punctuation* between the first and second sentences changes the meaning of ____________________ .

(the whole sentence) (the last word)

the whole sentence

86

We can recognize the difference between a statement and an exclamation. Telling someone "Go away!" is different from telling them "Go away." Write the example of an *exclamation* that you see in this frame.

____

Go away!

87

When you write a sentence that expresses an especially strong feeling or opinion, you should punctuate it with (a, an) ________________ .

exclamation mark (!)

88

It is even more obvious that when the sentence you are writing is a question, you should punctuate it with a question mark. Still, one of the most common mistakes people make when they write is ending questions with a period.

Which of the following sentences should end with a question mark? (*Check all that apply.*)

______ *a.* It is unbelievable that so much money was stolen.
______ *b.* Can you believe that so much money was stolen.
______ *c.* When will we see the end of all this misery.
______ *d.* It is easy to understand how this could have happened.
______ *e.* How could this have happened.

b, c, e

89

Now rewrite the two *nonquestions* from the previous frame as *questions*.

1. It is unbelievable that so much money was stolen.

____

____

2. It is easy to understand how this could have happened.

____

____

1. Is it unbelievable that so much money was stolen?
2. Is it easy to understand how this could have happened?

90

In the following paragraph, there are sentences that should be punctuated with question marks. Underline these sentences and then rewrite the paragraph, correcting the punctuation.

> The draft law is one of the most confusing laws in our country. Since very few lawyers understand it, is it any wonder that very few young men do. What are the reasons for this. One is that many legal decisions are left up to individual draft boards.

____

____

The draft law is one of the most confusing laws in our country. Since very few lawyers understand it, is it any wonder that very few young men do? What are the reasons for this? One is that many legal decisions are left up to individual draft boards.

91

The types of punctuation we have just illustrated—period, exclamation mark, and question mark—are used to *end* sentences. Other types of punctuation, like the *comma,* are used within sentences.

Circle the *comma* in the following sentence.

He sent us candy, cookies and fruit.

He sent us candy, cookies and fruit.

92

In the previous frame, the comma was used to separate items in a list. You should notice the option that no comma was necessary before or after the word "and." Use of a comma before the word "and" is a matter of personal perference. However, it is helpful to use the comma before "and" to avoid the effect of showing the last items in a list as combined. Look at the following example:

For lunch they served roast beef, ham, and peanut butter and jelly sandwiches.

Peanut butter and jelly is considered as one item.

93

Commas have other functions in a sentence besides separating items in a list. In a complex sentence, they follow a dependent clause when the dependent clause introduces the sentence.

Look at these two complex sentences:

1. The nurse wouldn't see me because I was not twenty-one.
2. Because I was not twenty-one, the nurse wouldn't see me.

Why is there a comma in sentence 2 and not in sentence 1?

(*Your own words*)

In sentence 1, the independent clause begins the sentence—so no comma is necessary. In sentence 2, the dependent clause begins the sentence—so it must be followed by a comma.

94

In compound sentences, commas should be used after the first independent clause (unless the sentence is very short, in which case it's up to you whether to use the comma or not). Look at the following example:

> I have learned to take good lecture notes, but I still have difficulty with textbook underlining.

Some of the following sentences are punctuated incorrectly. Rewrite *only* those sentences in which commas *must* be used.

1. He intended to take us to Vermont last Wednesday but his car broke down.

---

2. The first chapter was easy but the second was impossible.

---

3. I knew the meeting would turn out that way and I decided not to go for that reason.

---

1. He intended to take us to Vermont last Wednesday, but his car broke down.
3. I knew the meeting would turn out that way, and I decided not to go for that reason.

95

In some of the following sentences, commas are missing. Insert commas in these sentences where they are needed.

1. Because the storm lasted until Thursday we couldn't go to the shore.
2. He came and she refused to see him.
3. There were more than six of us requesting permission to speak but we were still locked out.
4. Of all the people who signed the petition only three came to the meeting.

1. Thursday, we
3. speak, but
4. petition, only

96

Commas should be used after: (*Check all that apply.*)

______ *a.* an independent clause that begins a complex sentence
______ *b.* a dependent clause that begins a complex sentence
______ *c.* an element of a list
______ *d.* a very short independent clause that begins a compound sentence

b, c

97

In the following paragraph, commas have been omitted in several places. Insert commas where necessary.

> The book is by a leading spokesman of the Algerian revolution but the author is not simply antiwhite. Since he is also a well-known black psychiatrist he is well qualified to understand the social psychological and personal turmoil involved in all social reorganization.

revolution, but
psychiatrist, he
social, psychological

98

A semicolon may be used in place of a comma and the connecting word in a compound sentence.

Look at the following sentences:

The first chapter was easy, but the second was impossible.

The first chapter was easy; the second was impossible.

I knew the meeting would turn out that way, and I decided not to go for that reason.

I knew the meeting would turn out that way; I decided not to go for that reason.

Use a semicolon in the following sentences:

1. Outlining helps to organize thoughts, and it is a helpful step in writing an essay.
2. The highways were crowded, and the traffic moved slowly.
3. Sandra was beautiful, but Martha was intelligent.

---

1. Outlining helps to organize thoughts; it is a helpful step in writing an essay.
2. The highways were crowded; the traffic moved slowly.
3. Sandra was beautiful; Martha was intelligent.

Whenever you reread compositions you have written, check them for all the common mistakes we have shown you in this unit. Once you have learned to avoid *obvious* problems, you will be in a position to develop a writing style which will help you to communicate with other people not only correctly but expressively.

99

A problem that students have when they write is the problem of capital letters. Almost everybody knows that sentences must begin with a capital letter, and yet students still make mistakes in capitalizing sentence beginnings.

Here are two things to remember to help you avoid these mistakes:

1. If a word is the first word of a sentence, it must begin with a capital letter.
2. If a group of words is *not* a complete sentence, capitalizing the first word in the group won't make it one.

Some of the following groups of words are complete sentences; some are not. Correct the use of capital letters. (A slash through a capital letter indicates that it should be lower case; three underscores beneath a lower-case letter indicate that it should be capitalized.)

1. they were shocked to hear the truth.
2. And then I said.
3. Did you faint?
4. if you need money, I can lend you some.
5. Because many of us.

---

1. they
   They were shocked to hear the truth.
2. And
   and then I said
3. Did you faint?
   (no correction necessary)
4. if
   If you need money, I can lend you some.
5. Because
   because many of us

100

Other words you should capitalize are:

1. proper nouns
2. proper adjectives

Compare the words in the columns below:

A	*B*
railroad station	Grand Central
river	Harlem River
park	Yellowstone
street	Broad Street

The words in column B are capitalized; those in column A are not. Column A names general things or places; column B names ________________ things or places. (general) (specific)

specific

(The words in column A are general names; the words in column B name *specific examples* of the words in column A.)

101

The words in *column B* in the previous frame (Grand Central, Harlem River, Yellowstone, Broad Street) are all *proper* nouns. You can see how proper nouns work by examining what happens when you name a *person.*

If you write, "my sister," you don't have to capitalize it. But if you write "my sister *Eileen,*" and *name* her, you must capitalize her name.

Rewrite the following sentence so that it is capitalized correctly.

please stop at my street, lark street.

____

Please stop at my street, Lark Street.

102

Rewrite the following sentences so that they are capitalized correctly.

1. of course i've seen an ocean—the atlantic ocean.

____

____

2. he lives in a small town named rogersville.

____

____

3. their friend on seventh avenue can drive tonight.

____

____

4. the map showed several countries: paraguay, chile, uruguay, and peru.

____

____

5. of all the doctors, doctor froman is the cheapest.

____

____

1. Of course I've seen an ocean—the Atlantic Ocean.
2. He lives in a small town named Rogersville.
3. Their friend on Seventh Avenue can drive tonight.
4. The map showed several countries: Paraguay, Chile, Uruguay, and Peru.
5. Of all the doctors, Doctor Froman is the cheapest.

103

Proper nouns generally fall into one of several categories: for example, names of days and months, geographical (place) names, organization names, and people's titles.

In the following examples mark the letters that should be capitalized as you were shown in frame 99.

1. january
2. arizona
3. xerox corporation
4. national student association
5. wednesday
6. she got sick on long island, not in the city.
7. janice works for xerox corporation as a secretary.
8. we listened to the secretary of state speak.
9. he isn't a citizen of any special state.

1. january
2. arizona
3. xerox corporation
4. national student association
5. wednesday
6. she got sick on long island, not in the city.
7. janice works for xerox corporation as a secretary.
8. we listened to the secretary of state speak.
9. he isn't a citizen of any special state.

104

In long titles or names (such as St. John's School for Girls), the shortest, least important words (usually connecting words, like *for*) are generally *not* capitalized.

Which of the following names is capitalized correctly? (*Check one.*)

______ *a.* the Hall Of Mirrors
______ *b.* The Hall of Mirrors
______ *c.* the Hall of Mirrors

c

105

Proper adjectives are derived from proper nouns and indicate specific kinds of persons, places, or things. They require capitalization.

Compare these two columns:

A	*B*
a wine from Spain	a Spanish wine
a penguin from Antarctica	an Antarctican penguin
a spy from Peru	a Peruvian spy
she speaks Italian	the Italian poetry

The words "Spain," "Antarctica," "Peru," and "Italian" in column A are capitalized because they are proper *nouns.* The capitalized words in column B are ________________

(nouns) (adjectives)

adjectives

106

In the previous frame, why do you think the words "Spanish," "Antarctican," "Peruvian," and "Italian" were capitalized?

___

___

"Spanish," "Antarctican," "Peruvian," and "Italian" *come from* proper nouns: Spain, Antarctica, Peru, Italy.

107

Write the proper *adjectives* that are derived from the following proper nouns:

NOUN	*ADJECTIVE*	
1. America	___	food
2. Cuba	___	scenery
3. Italy	___	symbolism

1. American
2. Cuban
3. Italian

108

The following sentences contain several mistakes in capitalization. Rewrite them so that they are correct.

1. When miss luce was a Child, she spoke only one Language.

   ___

2. several Doctors went to a conference in chile.

   ___

3. if my Sister could speak german, she would recite a Poem for you.

   ___

4. sister marie was the principal of st. john's school for girls.

   ___

1. When Miss Luce was a child, she spoke only one language.
2. Several doctors went to a conference in Chile.
3. If my sister could speak German, she would recite a poem for you.
4. Sister Marie was the principal of St. John's School for Girls.

109

Nouns and adjectives are called *proper* and are capitalized if they refer to:

____

____

(*Your own words*)

specific names or examples of persons, places, or things

Section 3 Word Order (Syntax)

Having skill at using words in the most precise and accurate order in sentences gives your reader the best opportunity to understand your intended meaning and enhances your style and readability as a writer. In this section of the text, we are going to show you the ways words should be ordered in sentences and the ways parts of speech function together.

There are four basic ways in which parts of speech function:

1. Nouns and pronouns have a naming function because they are used to name persons, places, or things.

2. Verbs have a doing function because they show what the naming words are doing and indicate at what time it is done.

3. Adjectives and adverbs have a modifying function because they modify, explain, clarify, or give qualities to the naming and doing words. Adjectives modify naming words; adverbs modify doing words. (Adverbs can also modify adjectives or other adverbs.)

4. Prepositions and conjunctions have a connecting function because they connect the other, more meaningful words to complete the sentence.

Of these parts of speech function categories, the first three mentioned are more important than the last. Modifiers are very important because they add dimension and vividness to the two major elements in the sentence, naming and doing words. The connectives link the three more important categories into a smooth flow of ideas.

To begin this section we are going to fill in slots that have been left blank in sentences which are part of a paragraph that tells a story. You will determine what the story is about by your selections. By doing the exercises, you should be able to discover a lot about word order patterns and about the way each part of speech functions in relation to other parts of the sentence.

Interjections, the eighth part of speech, are not presented here because their function is uniquely that of exclamation and they are readily identifiable in any sentence, for example, "gadzooks!"

Note also that the functions as identified here are at the most basic level, and will serve as a guide to structuring your syntax for most situations. When you have questions about applying these functions as your writing becomes more sophisticated, consult with your instructor.

Now, read through the following paragraphs. Fill in the blanks with words that seem to make sense in the sentences.

110

The ________________ ________________ woman went into the supermarket to do some ________________ shopping. Every eye followed her due to her ________________ appearance, which was heightened by her ________________ clothes. People began staring at her with such intensity that they were unaware of what ________________ things they were doing. Some shoppers were so preoccupied that they ran their carts into each other. All in all, it was a pretty ________________ situation. The ________________ ________________ woman certainly added a lot of excitement to what might have otherwise been a ________________ shopping day.

Type of Function: ____

Modifying words (adjectives)

111

Linda did everything at a snail's pace. Her lack of speed at getting dressed was ________________ driving her friends crazy. Even when Linda tried to make lists of things to help her get more organized and speed up, she couldn't compose it ________________ . We decided that she wasn't slow deliberately. The options of laziness and being lost in thought seemed ________________ the best motives we could identify for her behavior. Whatever the reasons, we've decided that she had better improve ________________ , or else. . . .

Type of function: ____

Modifying words (adverbs)

112

Early this morning as I stood in the ________________ an idea hit me. "I wonder what it would be like to become a ________________ ?" Here I was, a senior in college, and I still had no real idea of what to do for a ________________. I had tried a lot of ________________, but no one ________________ had made that big a(n) ________________ on me. Maybe my new idea would lead to my ________________ .

Type of function: ____

Naming words (nouns)

113

They never seemed to be able to stop studying. It was as if their every waking moment was devoted to school. In fact, school had so overtaken their lives that all ________________ spent their weekends on was homework. Thoughts of changing this life style often occurred to ________________, but in the final analysis ________________ were hooked on learning. He and she were known all over campus as talented students. He wanted to be a doctor, and ________________ wanted her Ph.D. in English. ________________ certainly appears that they will attain ________________ goals.

Type of function: ____

Naming words (pronouns)

114

Tom ________________ a marathon runner. He was always practicing and getting himself in shape for running long distances. He ________________ from class to class and never seemed to get tired. Students from all over the campus ________________ his constant training with amazement. If effort ________________ success, he should be a winner.

Type of function: ____

Doing words (verbs)

115

The incredible urge ____________ constantly eat had overcome me ____________ my first week ____________ college. The two words I learned ____________ call the urge were "the munchies." This overpowering need ____________ eat seemed most intense after I had been partying ____________ my friends. The effect got increasingly worse, the more I partied. My craving ____________ simple snacks like potato chips got accelerated ____________ mouth-watering mental images ____________ lobster and steak ____________ some exotic restaurant. My mind seems ____________ be stuck ____________ that point! I hope I can stop salivating and begin studying soon ____________ this galloping gourmet will be an ex-college student!!

Type of function: ____________________________

Connectives

Notice that, unlike the other three word categories, connectives do not have a marked effect on the meaning of the story.

116

Review the exercises that you have done in this section; notice that the naming word, which is the subject that the sentence is about, is located in the beginning part of the sentence. The doing word, which shows what the naming word/subject did, follows the naming word/subject in the sentence. Modifying words for the naming word are located near the naming word; modifying words for the doing word are located near the doing word. The connective words are located at places between the three more major word categories.

This typical sentence word order pattern could be illustrated as follows:

The overburdened	student	trudged	slowly	to	the	library.
Modifiers of naming word	Naming word subject	Doing word	Modifier of doing word	Connective	Modifier of naming word	Naming word

Through using a slightly different series of fill-in-the-slots exercises, we will now review what we have learned.

117

In the following sentences there will be slots for you to fill in as before. Also, there will be parentheses (   ) after each slot. After filling in the slot with a word of your choice, also identify what kind of function word it is in the parentheses provided. If the word is a particular kind of modifying or naming word, fill in the parentheses as follows: (modifier/adjective).

The coffee ________________ (   ) much too strong. Nevertheless, Fran tried ________________ (   ) drink it. ________________ (   ) was desperate to stay awake. The exam was scheduled for eight o'clock in the morning, and our smart but ________________ (   ) heroine had not yet started to study.

(doing word); (connecting word); (naming word/pronoun); (modifying word/adjective)

118

Create your own sentences using the same slot (parentheses) form as above. Try to follow this sequence in developing your first sentences: first, use a modifying word; second, use a naming word; third, use a connecting word; fourth, use a doing word. Notice what kinds of modifying and naming words this sequence creates.

Vary the sequence of function words in your following sentences; notice whether the location of the word affects which kind of naming and modifying word can be used. Also, notice whether it is possible to use all of the kinds of word function categories in the beginning of sentences; the middle; the end. When you have finished, review your findings with your instructor.

Sentence one:

____

____

____

Sentence two:

____

____

Sentence three:

____

____

Sentence four:

____

____

____

119

Keep this word order pattern in mind and you will help yourself immensely with word order precision. Especially remember that your writing is clearest to your reader when your modifiers are placed near the words you intend them to modify. For example, if words are not placed in the proper sequence it can make the word flow awkward and can affect the meaning of the following sentences.

a. Even Jack knew more about chess than Jill did.
b. Jack knew even more about chess than Jill did.

Which sentence implies that Jill didn't know very much about chess?

a

Which sentence implies that Jill knew a good bit about chess and Jack knew more?

b

Remember that your reader frequently uses the context of the whole sentence to understand what you are saying. Having words in appropriate order helps your meaning, your style, and the impact of your message on your reader.

120

Do the following exercise and notice the effect of word order on style and meaning.

a. Debbie, after the fact, learned about the chance for a vacation.
b. After the fact, Debbie learned about the chance for a vacation.
c. Learned about the chance for a vacation after the fact, Debbie?

Which of these word orders seems to express the idea most clearly?

b

Were all of the sentences meaningful?

Yes

121

Why does sentence *c* require a different mark of punctuation than the other two?

The unusual word order would only make sense as a question.

122

Create your own sentence, shift the word order around, and see whether the shifts affect your meaning and your style. When you have finished, review your sentences with your instructor.

Section 4 Grammatical Forms

Choosing the appropriate word form is crucial to both the style and the precision of meaning of the writer. When you finish this chapter, you should be able to select the appropriate grammatical forms in: writing parallel constructions; expressing time through verb tenses; using singular and plural number; describing through adjectives and adverbs; differentiating between subject and object pronouns; and showing possession or ownership.

Part 1
Parallelism

When you finish this segment of the book, you will be able to express *parallel* (related) ideas correctly in your writing. You will be able to avoid using faulty parallelism in verb phrases and in certain types of dependent clauses. (Refer back to section 1, frames 19 to 63 if you wish to review clauses.) You will practice writing sentences that use parallelism. At the end of the unit, you will correct and rewrite a paragraph containing faulty parallelism.

123

In sentences that use connecting words like "which" and "who" *one* of the ideas expressed in the sentences usually is more important than the other.

Look at this sentence:

> Mr. and Mrs. Abbott, who live in the mountains, sell handmade leather clothes.

Which is the *more* important statement this sentence makes about the Abbots?

a. The Abbotts live in the mountains.
b. The Abbots sell handmade leather clothes.

Answer ____________
(*a*) or (*b*)

b

124

Now compare these sentences:

a. The Abbotts, who live in the mountains, sell handmade leather clothes.
b. The Abbotts live in the mountains and sell handmade leather clothes.

Sentence *b* makes the same *statements* about the Abbotts that sentence *a* does. However, the *structure* of sentence *b* is different, and the difference in structure makes a difference in emphasis. In sentence *b*, the two statements about the Abbots have *equal* importance.

Go to the next frame.

No answer required.

125

Suppose you wanted to give *equal* emphasis or importance to *both* statements about the Abbotts. Which of the following sentences would you choose? (*Check the correct answer.*)

______ *a.* The Abbotts, who live in the mountains, sell handmade leather clothes.

______ *b.* The Abbotts, who sell handmade leather clothes, live in the mountains.

______ *c.* The Abbotts live in the mountains and sell handmade leather clothes.

c

126

The sentence, "The Abbotts live in the mountains and sell handmade leather clothes," has one *subject* and two *verbs.*

What are the two verbs?

________________ and ________________

live
sell

127

When the subject of a sentence has two verbs, *both* must agree with the subject.

Which of the following sentences is correct?

a. She sings and plays guitar in a local nightclub.
b. She sings and play guitar in a local nightclub.

Answer ____________
(*a*) or (*b*)

a

128

In sentences with more than one verb, there are other possible mistakes *besides* subject-verb agreement.

The following sentence is *wrong.*

His job is to write reports and filing them.

The verbs in this sentence, "to write" and "filing" are ________________ verb forms. (the same) (different)

different

129

If two verb forms in a sentence have the same emphasis and apply to the same subject, they should be in the same form, as in these examples:

a. He likes *to listen* to records and *to dance.*
b. We *are moving* to Chicago and (are) *selling* our house.

1. What are the two similar verbs in sentence *a*?

   _____ ________________ and _____ ________________

2. What are the two similar verbs in sentence *b*?

   _____ ________________ and (_____) ________________

1. to listen
   to dance
2. are moving
   (are) selling

130

Now look at this version of sentence *a* in the previous frame:

He likes *listening* to records and *to dance.*

This sentence is not good because the two related verbs ________________ in the same form. (are) (are not)

are not

131

You have seen that using these two verbs with the same subject is good: "to listen . . . to dance."

You have seen that using these verbs with the same subject is poor: "listening . . . to dance."

Which form of "dance" could you use with the verb "listening" when both have the same subject? (*Check the correct answer.*)

_______ *a.* to dance
_______ *b.* dances
_______ *c.* dancing

c

132

Fill in the blank in the sentence below, using the best form of "dance." Then write out your entire new sentence on the line provided.

He likes listening to records and _______________ with his girl friend.

____

dancing
He likes listening to records and dancing with his girl friend.

133

Which of the following sentences are better? (*Check all that apply.*)

_______ *a.* He likes *listening* to music and *to dance.*
_______ *b.* He likes *to listen* to music and *dancing.*
_______ *c.* He likes *listening* to music and *dancing.*
_______ *d.* He likes *to listen* to music and *to dance.*

c, d

134

You probably have noticed that when two closely related verbs are used in sentences like these, mistakes can be corrected in *two* ways. If the two verbs are in different forms (like "to listen" and "dancing"), you can change either one, as long as the two verb forms become the same.

Read this incorrect sentence:

He likes to smoke more than he likes drinking.

There are *two* ways to correct this sentence. On the lines below, write the two better sentences that you could make from this one. (*Hint: look back at frame 133 for help.*)

____

____

____

____

Either order:

He likes to smoke more than he likes to drink.
He likes smoking more than he likes drinking.

135

In the following sentences, fill in the blanks so that the verb forms are *parallel,* or the same.

1. Their idea of a vacation is *to drive* into the mountains and ________ (camping) ________ (to camp) there for a week.
2. I decided that leaving at dawn and ____________ (to drive) (driving) all day would be the best way to go.
3. We were able to argue with him and ____________ (to change) (changing) his mind.

1. to camp
2. driving
3. to change

You probably realize that people often leave out the second "to" in a parallel series: for example, "he likes to ride and swim." This doesn't mean that the verb forms aren't parallel. The sentence is a *shorter* version of "he likes to ride and *to swim.*"

136

The following sentence is not good.

She likes swimming and to water-ski.

Write the *two* possible better sentences that could be formed by changing the verb *forms.*

____

____

(Either order)

She likes to swim and to water-ski.
She likes swimming and water-skiing.

137

The following paragraph contains several examples of verb forms used incorrectly. *Rewrite* the paragraph so that they are better. (In some cases, there will be two possible better sentences. Use whichever possibility sounds better to you.)

Because housewives are often unable to work outside the home and are frequently forced performing unsatisfying chores, many are often tired, listless, and bored. A typical day may be spent in performing a never-ending series of tasks such as tidying the house, washing the dishes, changing the baby's diaper, and to prepare the dinner. The tasks are repetitious and never seem to be fully completed, thus bringing up the old adage, "a housewife's work is never done."

____

____

____

____

____

____

Because housewives are often unable to work outside the home and are frequently forced *to perform* unsatisfying chores, many are often tired, listless, and bored. A typical day may be spent in performing a never-ending series of tasks such as tidying the house, washing the dishes, changing the baby's diaper, and *preparing* the dinner. The tasks are repetitious and never seem to be fully completed, thus bringing up the old adage, "a housewife's work is never done."

138

The purpose of the United Nations is not to take the place of government actions or replacing traditional relations between countries. Its first purposes are to prevent arguments from becoming open war, and stopping any war that does break out. The next purposes are to develop a new morality among nations and creating an international community.

____
____
____
____
____
____
____
____

The purpose of the United Nations is not *to take* the place of government actions or *to replace* traditional relations between countries. (*or:* The purpose of the United Nations is not *taking* the place of government actions or *replacing* traditional relations between countries.) Its first purposes are *to prevent* arguments from becoming open war, and *to stop* any war that does break out. (*or:* Its first purposes are *preventing* arguments from becoming open war, and *stopping* any war that does break out.) The next purposes are *to develop* a new morality among nations and *to create* an international community. (*or:* The next purposes are *developing* a new morality among nations and *creating* an international community.)

139

To see more clearly what we mean by "two related ideas in a sentence," let's look at a *visual* example—one you can see.

You probably know what *parallel* lines are: lines like the sidewalks along a street or the rails of a railroad track. (For example, an equal-sign (=) consists of two parallel lines.)

When a sentence has two or more ideas so closely related that each helps to determine the other's meaning, they are called *parallel* ideas. Parallel ideas should *always* be expressed in similar word structure.

Which of these two sentences expresses *parallel* ideas? (*Check the correct answer.*)

______ *a.* In the summer she likes to swim and to water-ski.
______ *b.* In the summer she likes to swim.

a

140

Parallel ideas expressed in similar word structure are examples of *parallelism.*

Which of the following sentences contains an example of parallelism?

a. She asked us to buy her a drink.
b. She asked us to go to the bar and to buy her a drink.

Answer ____________
(*a*) or (*b*)

b

141

The sentences you corrected before, such as "He likes *to listen* to records and *dancing*," were examples of *bad parallelism.* The idea of listening to records is parallel to the idea of dancing—but the ideas are not expressed in a way that makes their relationship clear.

Let's take these two ideas:

a. studying for tests
b. worrying about grades

Obviously, these two ideas are closely related. If you want to use them together in a sentence in a way that shows their relationship, you should use parallel word structure.

Both of these sentences contain parallel ideas. Which of these sentences is correct?

a. It's no fun to study for tests or to worry about grades.
b. It's no fun studying for tests or to worry about grades.

Answer ____________
(*a*) or (*b*)

a

142

Which of the following sentences is correct?

a. He told us to get to work and that we should stop talking.
b. He told us to get to work and to stop talking.

Answer ___________
(*a*) or (*b*)

b

143

Obviously, parallelism does apply to more than verbs. For instance, the first example in the previous frame pointed out the fact that you can tell a person *to do* something, and you can tell a person *that he should* do something. But you shouldn't tell him both ways in the same sentence!

Is this sentence correct?

He told us that *The Exorcist* was a good movie and to see it.

Answer ___________
(yes) (no)

no

144

Fill in the space below so that the sentence will have the same *meaning* but will express it better.

He told us that *The Exorcist* was a good movie and

____

(that we should see it) (to see it)

He told us that *The Exorcist* was a good movie, and that we should see it.

145

Now read this sentence:

I told Mrs. Price that he has a wild imagination and not to believe everything he says.

Rewrite this sentence so that it is better.

____

____

I told Mrs. Price that he has a wild imagination and that she should not believe everything he says.

146

The following sentences are partially completed. Using the ideas in parentheses, *complete* the sentences so that they are clear and correct. (*Write your complete sentences on the lines below.*)

1. She says that their prices are too high and (we can't afford tickets).

 ____

2. He enjoys buying old furniture and (refinish it).

 ____

3. I like reading about different astrological signs and (apply it) to the people I know.

 ____

4. Her job is to entertain guests and (keep them happy).

 ____

1. She says that their prices are too high and that we can't afford tickets.
2. He enjoys buying old furniture and refinishing it.
3. I like reading about different astrological signs and applying what I've read to the people I know.
4. Her job is to entertain guests and to keep them happy.

147

Earlier, you were shown the following incorrect sentence.

He likes to smoke more than he likes drinking.

You saw that there were two ways of making the verb forms in this sentence parallel. Now look at the following sentence, in which verb forms are not the problem.

The director told us that we should pay more attention to him and to read our scripts more carefully.

Which of the following sentences are better versions of this sentence? (*Check all that apply.*)

______ *a.* The director told us to pay more attention to him and that we should read our scripts more carefully.

______ *b.* The director told us to pay more attention to him and to read our scripts more carefully.

______ *c.* The director told us that we should pay more attention to him and that we should read our scripts more carefully.

b, c

148
Write *two* possible better versions of this sentence:

I told him that he should stop talking and to leave.

I told him to stop talking and to leave.
I told him that he should stop talking and that he should leave.

149
Just as there can be any number of lines parallel to each other, there can also be any number of parallel ideas in a sentence.

Look at this example:

My brother-in-law is a domineering father, an ungrateful son, a rude husband, a worthless friend, and a terrible brother-in-law.

What are the parallel ideas in this sentence?

a domineering father
an ungrateful son
a rude husband
a worthless friend
a terrible brother-in-law

150
In the last frame, all five parallel ideas were expressed *correctly* in the same structure.

Which idea in this sentence is *not* expressed in parallel structure? (*Write the idea in the line below.*)

My brother-in-law is a domineering father, an ungrateful son, a rude husband, a worthless friend, and nobody likes him.

____

nobody likes him

151
Now look at the following incorrect sentence.

He was sympathetic, understanding, and people respected him.

Which of the following sentences would be a *correct* version of this sentence? (*Check the correct answer.*)

______ *a.* He was sympathetic, understanding, and a respected man.
______ *b.* He was sympathetic, understanding, and respected man.
______ *c.* He was sympathetic, understanding, and respected.

c

152
A common mistake that people make is to add *clauses* at the end of the lists of parallel "words."

What is wrong with this sentence?

The police asked their names, addresses, and what they were doing here.

____

(*Your own words*)

A clause—"what they were doing here"—is added to the end of a list of parallel *nouns*.

153
Look at this incorrect sentence.

He knows all the restaurants, nightclubs, and where to go.

Which of the following sentences is a correct version of this sentence? (*Check the correct answer.*)

_______ *a.* He knows all the restaurants, nightclubs, and where we should go.
_______ *b.* He knows all the restaurants, nightclubs, and places to go.
_______ *c.* He knows all the restaurants, nightclubs, and where the good places are.

b
(Sentence *b* is correct because it uses the word "places," a noun, to end a list of parallel nouns.)

154
Rewrite the following sentences so that the parallelism is good.

1. Their nightclub is small, crowded, and filled with smoke.

____

2. During exam time, he becomes tense, tired, irritable, and worries.

____

3. I read the beginning, the 4th chapter, and how it ended.

____

1. Their nightclub is small, crowded, and smoky.
2. During exam time, he becomes tense, tired, irritable, and worried.
3. I read the beginning, the 4th chapter, and the ending.

155
The following paragraph contains several examples of poor parallelism. Rewrite the paragraph so that it is correct.

Skiing is not as easy as it looks. A novice skier is advised to begin off the slope and learning about skiing equipment. She should know the difference between various types of skis, the care and maintenance of skiing equipment, and where to buy or rent it. Only then should she attempt to brave the slopes and working on developing her balance, coordination, reflexes, and how to be patient. Long hours of practice, numerous falls, and when your muscles get sore should pay off and a good skier should emerge.

____

____

____

____

____

____

____

____

Skiing is not as easy as it looks. A novice skier is advised to begin off the slope and *to learn* about skiing equipment. She should know the difference between various types of skis, the care and maintenance of skiing equipment, and *its place of purchase or rental.* Only then should she attempt to brave the slopes and *to work* on developing her balance, coordination, reflexes, and *patience.* Long hours of practice, numerous falls, and *sore muscles* should pay off and a good skier should emerge.

Parallel word structure is a very useful way of expressing ideas which are related. You should be careful, though, not to try to squeeze unrelated ideas into parallel form. It may be better to write two separate sentences than to confuse people by using parallelism in a misleading way.

Part 2
Verb Tenses

When you finish this segment of the book, you will be able to express *time* in your writing by using correct verb forms. You will be able to use the three main verb tenses to express past, present, and future time. You will be able to use singular and plural subjects with the correct singular and plural verbs.

156

If you were going to fill in the following blank spaces with verbs, which *form* of the verb would you need: a *present* form, or a *past* form?

1. I ______ him yesterday.

   Answer ________________
   (present) (past)

2. I ______ him now.

   Answer ________________
   (present) (past)

1. past
2. present

157

All verbs have both a present and a past form. Decide for each of these sample sentences which verb *form* is required.

1. I ________________ him the money last week.
   (present) (past)

2. Right now she ________________ .
   (present) (past)

3. Yesterday I ________________ .
   (present) (past)

4. I always visit him when I ________________ .
   (present) (past)

1. past
2. present
3. past
4. present

158

In each of the sentences in the last frame, there were clues to tell you which verb form was required.

Write down or explain what clue in each sentence told you whether to answer "past" or "present."

1. ______________________________
2. ______________________________
3. ______________________________
4. ______________________________

1. last week
2. now
3. Yesterday
4. "I always visit" is happening in the present, so the next verb must happen in the present too.

159

Look at the following list of sentences that use verbs in the *present* tense:

SUBJECT		*PRESENT TENSE VERB*	
1.	I	carry	it with me.
2.	We	run	too fast for them to catch up.
3.	I	hit	very few pins when I bowl.
4.	They	trade	in their cars every six years.

Now look at the same sentence again, this time with the verbs changed to the *past* tense:

SUBJECT		*PAST TENSE VERB*	
1.	I	carried	it home with me.
2.	We	ran	too fast for them to catch up.
3.	I	hit	very few pins when I bowled.
4.	They	traded	in their cars every six years.

Compare the different verb forms. Is there *one rule* that would account for all the verb changes involved?

Answer ____________
(yes) (no)

no

160

Look at the sentences numbered 4 in the last frame:

PRESENT: They *trade* in their cars every six years.
PAST: They *traded* in their cars every six years.

You can tell from reading these two sentences how important it is for a writer to make his verb tenses correct. There would be no way for you to know which of these sentences was in the past tense if the verb form were wrong.

The *past tense* of "trade" is formed by adding the letter ______ to the verb "trade."

-d

161

Most verbs are changed to the past tense by adding *-d* or *-ed.* For verbs like "trade" that end in *-e,* you only have to add ______ . For other verbs, add ____________
(*-d*) (*-ed*)

-d
-ed

162

Change the verbs in the following sentences to the past tense by adding *-d* or *-ed.*

1. Some of the children (behave) __________________ well.
2. I (wait) __________________ at least an hour for him.
3. The four of us (paint) __________________ the room in one night.

1. behaved
2. waited
3. painted

163

Change the verbs in the following sntences to the *present* tense.

1. The drama group (acted) ________________ well in front of an audience.
2. Debbie and Greg (danced) ________________ well together.
3. Only six of us regularly (attended) ________________ the meetings.

1. acts
2. dance
3. attend

164

In your own words, how are *most* verbs changed to the past tense?

____

by adding *-d* or *-ed*

165

Many verbs are *not* changed to the past tense by adding *-d* or *-ed*. For example, look at the following:

begin/began   stand/stood   throw/threw

These verbs are not changed to the past tense according to any rule. You would learn the past tenses of such verbs through your day-to-day reading and writing experience.

Let's get an idea how you stand on the past tenses of some of these *irregular*, or unusual verbs. In the blank to the right of each of the present tense verbs below, write the *past* tense.

1. give ______
2. bring ______
3. swim ______
4. is ______
5. come ______
6. drive ______
7. drink ______
8. eat ______
9. go ______
10. stand ______
11. fight ______
12. see ______
13. say ______
14. do ______
15. hit ______
16. read ______
17. run ______
18. make ______
19. break ______
20. tell ______

1.	gave	8.	ate	15.	hit
2.	brought	9.	went	16.	read
3.	swam	10.	stood	17.	ran
4.	was	11.	fought	18.	made
5.	came	12.	saw	19.	broke
6.	drove	13.	said	20.	told
7.	drank	14.	did		

If you had more than five errors in the previous frame, spend about ten minutes reading the past tenses of these verbs.

When you finish, go to frame 166. For the rest of the program refer to this list whenever you are in doubt about the past tense of a verb.

If you had fewer than five errors, go to frame 166.

166

The most important thing to remember about writing verb tenses is to use the tense that is consistent with the time expressed by the rest of the sentence.

Explain what is confusing about this sentence:

I *give* him the money *yesterday*.

____

____

The verb is in the present tense but the sentence refers to the past ("yesterday").

167

Correct the sentence "I give him the money yesterday" by making the verb tense correct. (*Write your new sentence on the lines provided.*)

____

____

I gave him the money yesterday.

168

There are, of course, other ways to express past and present besides the simple present and the simple past we have been working with.

Look at these sentences:

Right now I *am working* on a project.
He *is making* a phone call and can't be disturbed.
We *are wondering* where they could be.

These sentences all express ________________ time.
(past) (present)

present

169

Verb forms like *am going, is throwing,* and *are quitting* are in the "present progressive" tense. This means that the activity is still going on (in progress) as of the writing of the sentence.

Read these sentences:

a. Randolph jogs for one hour each day.
b. In fact, he is jogging right now.
c. In this class, we study journalism.
d. We are now studying journalism in this class.

1. Sentence *a* uses the ____________________ present tense.
(simple) (progressive)
2. Sentence *b* uses the ____________________ present tense.
(simple) (progressive)
3. Sentence *c* uses the ____________________ present tense.
(simple) (progressive)
4. Sentence *d* uses the ____________________ present tense.
(simple) (progressive)

1. simple
2. progressive
3. simple
4. progressive

170

Rewrite the following sentences using the present progressive form of the verb.

1. He studies diligently.

   ____

2. He works hard.

   ____

1. He is studying diligently.
2. He is working hard.

171

The present progressive is most useful in speaking. You probably will not use the present progressive tense very often when you write.

However, you probably will want to use the past progressive tense in your writing. Compare these two sentences:

He is reading.
He was reading.

Which of these sentences is in the past progressive tense? (*Write the sentence in the blank below.*)

____

He was reading.

172

The past progressive is useful in relating someone's (or your own) experience step by step as it happened.

The following paragraph describes an accident. Write in the blanks the past progressive form of the verbs in the parentheses.

"I (drive) ______________ down First Street behind a truck. The light (change) ______________ but I couldn't see it because of the truck. By the time I realized I (run) ______________ a red light, the other car (crunch) ______________ into the side of my car."

was driving
was changing
was running
was crunching

173

Rewrite the following sentences using the past progressive form of the verb.

1. He studied all evening for the exam.
2. He read the newspaper page by page.

1. He was studying all evening for the exam.
2. He was reading the newspaper page by page.

Another verb form that is sometimes useful in writing is the emphatic. This form is used to emphasize the verb; like the progressive tense, it has both past and present forms. The verb "do" plus the main verb creates the emphatic verb form.

Look at these sentences.

I do believe he does work.
We do attend the meetings.

1. These sentences are examples of the ________________ emphatic.
(past) (present)

Now look at these sentences.

I did believe he did work.
We did attend the meetings.

2. These sentences are examples of the ________________ emphatic.
(past) (present)

1. present
2. past

174

In changing from the present emphatic to the past emphatic, which verb changed—"do" or the main verb?

____

do

Rewrite the following sentences, using the emphatic forms of the verb.

1. I think he passed the test.
2. We work well together.

1. I do think he did pass the test.
2. We do work well together.

175

We have learned three ways of expressing past and present time. In each of the following situations, write a sentence using the correct verb tense to express time.

1. Use the *simple present tense.*
   They (call) me every day.

   ____

2. Use the *simple past tense.*
   He (invite) us yesterday.

   ____

3. Use the *present emphatic tense.*
   It's true that they (bore) me.

   ____

4. Use the *past emphatic tense.*
   He doesn't believe me, but I (give) her the money.

   ____

5. Use the *present progressive tense.*
   I (do) this only as a favor to you.

   ____

6. Use the *past progressive tense.*
   I (talk) about him when I saw him behind me.

   ____

1. They *call* me every day.
2. He *invited* us yesterday.
3. It's true that they *do bore* me.
4. He doesn't believe me, but I *did give* her the money.
5. I *am doing* this only as a favor to you.
6. I *was talking* about him when I saw him behind me.

176

In some of the following sentences there are verb tense errors. *Rewrite only the incorrect sentences,* using the *correct* verbs.

1. Yesterday we do give him his money, but today we didn't.

   ____

2. The arena is full when we arrived.

   ____

3. Usually, only half the drivers finish the race.

   ____

4. I am just too busy to help you.

   ____

5. The teacher did get mad when students are late for class.

   ____

6. He dates at least three girls at a time.

   ____

7. He is going home when we saw him last week.

   ____

8. The sun was coming up as we left the party.

   ____

9. I do help him once, but never again.

   ____

10. He came in because I was playing his favorite record.

   ____

1. Yesterday we *did give* him his money, but today we didn't.
2. The arena *was* full when we arrived.
5. The teacher *does get* mad when students are late for class.
7. He *was going* home when we saw him last week.
9. I *did help* him once, but never again.

177

There is one other basic verb tense—the *future* tense.

If the past tense is used to describe events that *have* happened or *were* happening, and the present tense is used to describe events that *happen* or *are* happening, then the future tense is used to describe events that ______________ .

will happen

178
If your answer to the previous frame was "will happen," you were using the *future tense.*

Examine the following sentences:

She *will go* next week.
George *will leave* soon.
Class *will be* over soon.
We *will wait* a little while longer.

What is the one word in the sentences above that indicates the future tense when it is placed in front of the main verb?

____

will

179
In the following paragraph, change the verbs in parentheses to *future* tense.

New relationships (arise) _______________ between husbands and wives. For example, there always (be) _______________ certain differences between men and women. However, the institutions that create these differences (change) _______________ , and the human couple (make) _______________ an adjustment.

will arise
will be
will change
will make

180
Rewrite the following sentences, using the *future* tense of the verbs in parentheses.

1. He always says he (call), but he never does.

   ____

2. Do you think the concert (begin) on time?

   ____

1. He always says he will call, but he never does.
2. Do you think the concert will begin on time?

181
The following sentences use the *progressive* form of the verb "read." Look them over and then answer the question below.

1. He was reading.
2. He is reading.
3. He will be reading.

What *tense* is each of these sentences?

1. ________________ progressive
2. ________________ progressive
3. ________________ progressive

1. past
2. present
3. future

182
Use the correct example of the progressive tenses in rewriting each of these sentences.

1. He (drive) yesterday.

   ____

2. Ellen (drive) today.

   ____

3. I (drive) tomorrow.

   ____

1. He was driving yesterday.
2. Ellen is driving today.
3. I will be driving tomorrow.

183
Rewrite the following sentence using the future progressive form of the verb.

1. He will pay me back in monthly installments.

   ____

1. He will be paying me back in monthly installments.

184

Examine these two sentences:

1. He did sleep.
2. He does sleep.

Would it be possible to write a third sentence, using the emphatic form in the future tense?

Answer ___________
(yes) (no)

no

185

Now let's review the three basic tenses we have learned. Look over the chart that follows and the examples given for each tense.

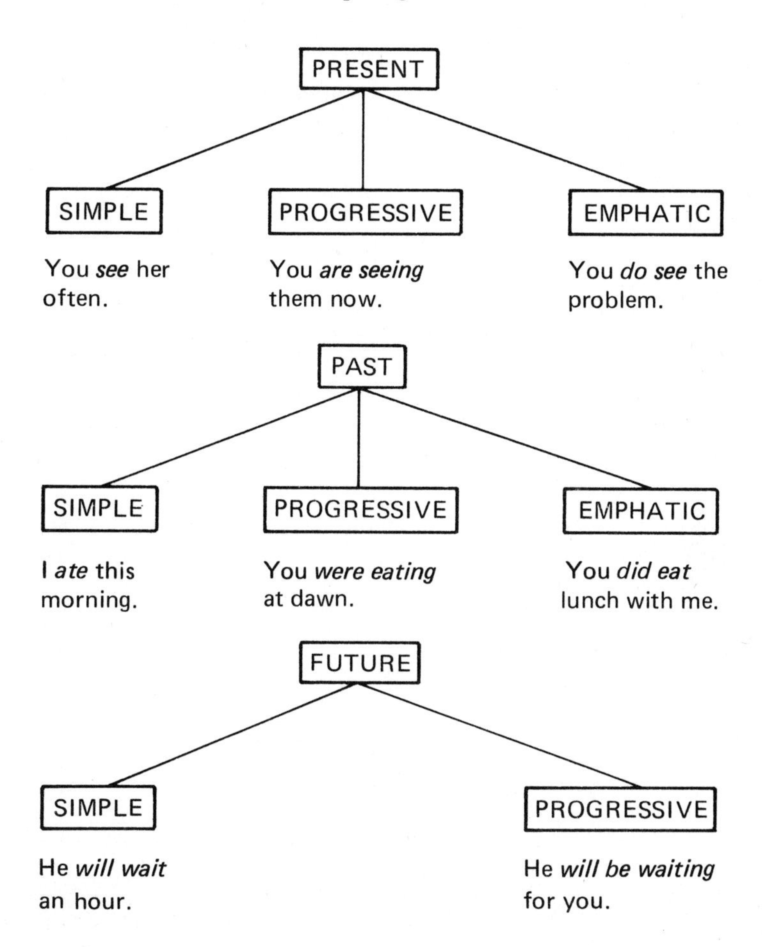

no answer required

The reason for learning the different verb tenses is to be able to indicate clearly what *time* you are writing about.

Most of your writing will be in the form of paragraphs. Therefore, you need to know how to apply your knowledge of verb tenses to paragraph writing.

186

Some people think that once a paragraph is started in a particular verb tense, that tense should be continued throughout the paragraph. This is not necessarily so. Verb tenses within a paragraph depend on the time expressed in each idea in the paragraph.

Read through the following paragraph. Notice how the verb tenses change to fit the meaning of the paragraph.

> Talking to my history teacher is like talking to a brick wall! Yesterday I told him that I needed more time in which to complete my term paper, but he did not even seem to hear me. I am currently still working on it, but I doubt if it will be completed by tomorrow.

Notice how the verb tense changed, depending on the time expressed in each idea in the paragraph.

187

In many cases, words like "now," "currently," "yesterday," "tomorrow," and "previously" will decide the verb tense to be used.

Each of the following examples calls for a certain verb tense in the blanks next to the key words, write the *time* that each expresses (past, present, or future).

For example: now ______ present ______

1. at the moment ______
2. currently ______
3. yesterday ______
4. tomorrow ______
5. previously ______
6. last night ______
7. in the next year ______
8. formerly ______

1. present
2. present
3. past
4. future
5. past
6. past
7. future
8. past

188

Read through the following paragraph. Circle any verb whose tense you think is incorrect.

> I was looking forward to summer vacation. I spend last summer down at the shore, but this year, I is planning to spend some time camping in the mountains. I is presently saving my money so that in the future I am able to take a trip to Europe.

I *was looking* forward to
I *spend* last summer
I *is spending* some time camping
I *is* presently *saving* my money
I *am able* to take a trip.

189

Rewrite the paragraph so that it is correct.

____

____

____

____

I am looking forward to summer vacation. I spent last summer down at the shore, but this year, I am planning to spend some time camping in the mountains. I am presently saving my money so that in the future I will be able to take a trip to Europe.

190

Now write your own paragraph using all three tenses (past, present, future). Include the following details in your paragraph: arriving at school late, missing first class, explaining the situation to your instructor. Have your instructor review your paragraph with you.

Now we'll go on to some more complicated time relationships.

191

What time (past, present, or future) do the three verb forms below express?

I waited an hour.
I have waited an hour.
I had waited an hour.

Answer ______________________

(past) (present) (future)

past

192

All three of the verbs in the last frame express *past* time. But only one is an example of the *simple* past tense that you saw in the paragraph you corrected.

Look again at the three verbs:

I waited.
I have waited.
I had waited.

Which of these are *not* examples of the *simple* past tense?

____

____

193

Neither "have waited" nor "had waited" is an example of the *simple* past tense. Yet, they both refer to past actions.

Read the following sentences carefully.

a. I have waited an hour for him.
b. I had waited an hour by the time he finally called.

Sentence *a* has *one* verb that expresses past time, but sentence *b* has *two*: "had waited" and "called." Which of the following situations describes the relationship between these two verbs correctly? (*Check the correct answer.*)

_______ *a.* I had waited an hour *after* he called.
_______ *b.* I had waited *the* moment he *called.*
_______ *c.* I waited an hour *before* he *called.*

c

194
The verb "have waited" says only that you waited *some* time in the past and are still waiting. The verb "had waited" says that you waited at or for a definite time _______________ something else happened.
(before) (after)

before

195
Look at this example:

she broke four windows/the teacher finally stopped her

Which of these two events happened *first*?

____

she broke four windows

196
In the blank below, write the word that will make it clear that the window breaking happened *first.* (*Look back to the previous frame if necessary.*)

She __________ broken four windows when the teacher finally stopped her.
(had) (has)

had

197
Now compare these two sentences:

a. The skier has fallen twice already.
b. The skier had fallen twice already by the time the ski patrol reached him.

Sentence *b* contains two verbs: "had fallen" and "reached."

Which of the actions that these verbs describe happened *first*? (*Reread the sentence to find your answer.*)

Answer ______________________
(had fallen) (reached)

had fallen

198

The sentence, "The skier had fallen twice already by the time the ski patrol reached him," *means* that: (*Check the correct answer.*)

_____ *a.* The skier fell twice *after* the ski patrol reached him.
_____ *b.* The skier fell twice *before* the ski patrol reached him.
_____ *c.* neither of the above.

b

199

1. Which of the following verb forms would refer to something that happened at some indefinite time in the past?

   Answer ______________________
   (has fallen) (had fallen)

2. Which of the following verb forms would refer to something that happened *prior* to another *past* event?

   Answer ______________________
   (has fallen) (had fallen)

1. has fallen
2. had fallen

200

"Have (*or* has) fallen" and "had fallen" are examples of two different verb tenses.

1. "Have (*or* has) fallen" uses the ______________ tense of *have* plus the main verb. (past) (present)
2. "Had fallen" uses the ______________ tense of *have* plus the main verb. (past) (present)

1. present
2. past

201

Fill in the blanks in the following sentences with the *correct* form of *have.*

1. I ______________ told you about him often.
   (have) (had)
2. They ______________ already fallen 10 feet by the time we caught them.
   (have) (had)
3. Before we pointed out the mistake, she ______________ already printed fifty copies.
   (has) (had)
4. We ______________ taken our exams already.
   (have) (had)
5. We ______________ arrived at school just in time for first class.
   (have) (had)

1. have
2. had
3. had
4. have
5. had

202

Fill in the blanks below with the correct tense of the verb "wait."

1. He ______________ an hour by the time the package arrived.
2. He ______________ long enough.

1. had waited
2. has waited

203

"Had waited" is an example of the *past perfect* tense.

"Have (or has) waited" is an example of the *present perfect* tense.

When you want to describe an action that happened *before* a related past action, you should use the ______________ tense.

past perfect

204

1. The present perfect tense is formed by the ______________ tense of "have" plus the main verb.
(present) (past)

2. The past perfect tense is formed by the ______________ tense of "have" plus the main verb.
(present) (past)

1. present
2. past

205

The sentences below were given in an earlier frame. Compare them again.

a. The skier has fallen twice already.
b. The skier had fallen twice already by the time the ski patrol reached him.

1. Sentence ______________ contains the *present perfect* tense of "fall."
(*a*) or (*b*)

2. Sentence ______________ contains the *past perfect* tense of "fall."
(*a*) or (*b*)

1. *a*
2. *b*

206

You know that most verbs have different forms for the simple *past* tense and the simple *present* tense (for example, I *run,* I *ran*). Many verbs also have a different form for the *perfect* tenses.

Look at the following examples of the verb "fall":

I *fall.*
I *fell.*
I have *fallen.*
I had *fallen.*

Which form of the verb "fall" is used for the *perfect* tenses?

____

fallen

207

Most verbs that form their past tense by adding *-d* or *-ed* also form their perfect tenses by adding *-d* or *-ed.*

Write the *present perfect* tense of the verb "use" to complete this sentence.

He ________________ that same car for many years.

has used

208

However, many verbs do *not* form their perfect tenses by adding *-d* or *-ed.*

Read through these examples of perfect tenses.

I have begun	you have given
he had thrown	they had come
we have seen	Shirley has done

Is there any one rule you can observe that could account for all these forms?

Answer ____________
(yes) (no)

no

The only way to learn the *perfect* forms of verbs like these is to watch for them in your own reading and writing. Often, grammar books give you lists of the different verb forms, and the *perfect* forms will often be found listed under the name *perfect participle* or *past participle.* Until you are sure of the right forms to use, consult lists like these whenever you write, or look up the verb in a dictionary.

Go to the next frame.

209

When you look up a verb in a dictionary, the dictionary will generally list the simple present, simple past, perfect participle, and present participle (-ing form). Often the simple past and the perfect participle are the *same.* In such cases, the dictionary will not repeat the form but will list it only *once.*

Suppose, in a paper you are writing, you get stuck on the verb "fall" because you can't remember the perfect form. You look it up, and find "fell, fallen, falling."

1. Which of the above is the *perfect* form of "fall"?

   ____

2. Suppose you look up "submit" and find "submitted, submitting." What is the *perfect* form of "submit"?

____

1. fallen
2. submitted

210

Compare these two columns of verbs:

PERFECT	*PAST*
I have seen	I saw
you had been	you were
he had done	he did

Which of the above tenses *must* have a form of "have" before the main verb?

Answer _______________
(perfect) (past)

perfect

211

One of the most common mistakes that people make (especially in *speaking* English) is using the *perfect* form of a verb *without* a form of "have."

What is wrong with this sentence?

She done a good job.

____

____

____

(*Your own words*)

The verb "has" is missing, "done" is used alone, "done" is not the past tense, and so on.

212
These two sentences are *correct* versions of "She done a good job."

a. She *has done* a good job.
b. She *did* a good job.

Write two *correct* versions of this sentence: I been lonely.

____

____

(Either order)

I *have been* lonely.
I *was* lonely.

213
Write two correct versions of this sentence: I seen the whole thing.

____

____

(Either order)

I *have seen* the whole thing.
I *saw* the whole thing.

214
Using the *simple past* tense, rewrite the following *incorrect* sentences.

1. He been here three days.

   ____

2. They seen him only once.

   ____

3. Did he say we arrive too soon?

   ____

1. He was here three days.
2. They saw him only once.
3. Did he say we arrived too soon?

215

Now, using the *present perfect* tense, rewrite the same incorrect sentences.

1. He been here three days.

____

2. They seen him only once.

____

3. Did he say we arrive too soon?

____

1. He has been here three days.
2. They have seen him only once.
3. Did he say we have arrived too soon?

We've seen examples of three kinds of verb mistakes that you should watch out for:

1. using the present perfect *instead of* the past perfect to express something that happened before some other past event;
2. using the wrong form of the main verb in perfect tenses; and
3. using perfect verb forms without a form of "have."

Now we'll correct some sentences that contain these mistakes.

Go to the next frame.

216

Rewrite these sentences so that they are correct.

1. I have been at home a week when the letter arrived.

____

____

2. By the time he finally called, she gone to bed.

____

____

3. They wanted to ask you, but earlier you have said you were too busy.

____

____

1. I *had been* home a week when the letter arrived.
2. By the time he finally called, she *had gone* to bed.
3. They wanted to ask you, but earlier you *had said* you were too busy.

217

Rewrite these sentences so that they are correct.

1. Professor Brown has want to meet you.

 ____

2. We have already began the experiment.

 ____

3. He had anticipate your question.

 ____

1. Professor Brown has *wanted* to meet you.
2. We have already *begun* the experiment.
3. He had *anticipated* your question.

218

The following paragraph contains several of the errors we have just corrected. Read through the paragraph and circle the incorrect verbs.

> Ellen is going out with the most gorgeous man I ever seen! She likes him so much that she had stopped seeing her old boyfriend. I'm really glad that she is so happy, but I can't help wishing that I have seen him first.

seen
had stopped
have seen

219

Rewrite the paragraph in the previous frame, this time using the correct verb forms.

____

____

____

____

Ellen is going out with the most gorgeous man I have ever seen! She likes him so much that she has stopped seeing her old boyfriend. I'm really glad that she is so happy, but I can't help wishing that I had seen him first.

220

Rewrite the following paragraph using the correct past tense of the verb in parentheses.

I ________________ (see) New York City for the first time two weeks ago. I ________________ (have) visited friends in New Jersey that day and decided to stop in the city on my way home. When I got off the train at Pennsylvania Station, I was amazed because I ________________ (have) never before seen a place so crowded. After I had ________________ (walk) up and down Thirty-fourth Street for a few minutes, I decided that I should have ________________ (wait) to visit New York until fewer people were there.

____

____

____

____

____

____

____

____

I *saw* New York City for the first time two weeks ago. I *had* visited friends in New Jersey that day and decided to stop in the city on my way home. When I got off the train at Pennsylvania Station, I was amazed because I *had* never before seen a place so crowded. After I had *walked* up and down Thirty-fourth Street for a few minutes, I decided that I should have *waited* to visit New York until fewer people were there.

221

There is one more "perfect" tense besides the present perfect and past perfect.

Look at the three tense forms of "have" italicized below:

a. you *had* gone
b. you *have* given
c. you *will have* taken

1. Verb *a* uses the _______________ tense form of "have."
2. Verb *b* uses the _______________ tense form of "have."
3. Verb *c* uses the _______________ tense form of "have."

1. past
2. present
3. future

222

"You had gone," "you have given," and "you will have taken" illustrate *three perfect tenses.*

1. "You had gone" is in the _______________ perfect tense.
2. "You have given" is in the _______________ perfect tense.
3. "You will have taken" is in the _______________ perfect tense.

1. past
2. present
3. future

223

Read these two related clauses:

they *will have made* a decision already / by the time we get to the meeting.

Of the two events described here, which will happen *first*? (*Write out the entire clause.*)

____

they will have made a decision already

224

The following sentences illustrate the *future perfect* tense. Read them carefully.

She *will have gone* by the time the train comes.
That dress *will have gone* out of style before you finish it.
I *will have come* and *gone* before he sees me.
Will they *have decided* the verdict by the end of the day?

The *future perfect* tense is used to describe an action which: (*Check the correct answer.*)

______ *a.* will happen *after* a specified future event.
______ *b.* will happen *before* a specified future event.
______ *c.* happened *before* a specified past event.

b. will happen *before* a specified future event

(If you answered (*a*), read the sentences again. If you answered (*c*), you are thinking of the *past* perfect tense.)

225

Rewrite each of the following sentences in the future perfect tense.

For example: He (gone) by the time I get home.

Answer: *He will have gone by the time I get home.*

1. I (given) him the money by two o'clock today.

____

2. Did he say that he (flunked out) by June of this year?

____

3. I (paid) for my car on April 1 of next year.

____

1. I *will have* given him the money by two o'clock today.
2. Did he say that he *will have* flunked out by June of this year?
3. I *will have* paid for my car on April 1 of next year.

226

Here is an example of a problem to watch out for in *all* perfect tenses.

Read this sentence carefully:

I have *written* a story and *given* it to the editor.

This sentence is *correct.* You might have thought that the verb "given" should have been preceded by the word "have"—as in a sentence like "I have given him a ride." However, in sentences with *two verbs* in the same perfect tense that refer to the same subject, the second "have" is often dropped.

I have written a story and *have* given it to the editor.
I have written a story and given it to the editor.

227

Rewrite the following sentences, using the *correct* form of the verbs in parentheses.

1. He had come and (go) by midnight.

____

____

2. We have tried and (try) to convince him.

____

____

3. You will have given up and (leave) by the time they call.

____

____

1. He had come and *gone* by midnight.
2. We have tried and *tried* to convince him.
3. You will have given up and *left* by the time they call.

228

The following paragraph contains several mistakes in the perfect tenses. Rewrite it so that it is correct.

Choosing a college major is rough. I have completed all my required courses before I even began to think about my major. I has finally decided on psychology, and has registered for fifteen credits for the fall semester. By the end of this year, I had completed sixty credits altogether.

Choosing a college major is rough. I had completed all my required courses before I even began to think about my major. I have finally decided on psychology, and have registered for fifteen credits for the fall semester. By the end of this year, I will have completed sixty credits altogether.

229

The following paragraph contains several mistakes in verb tenses. Rewrite it so that it is correct.

> School had really broadened my horizons. It seems as if lately most of my free time had been spent in reading; not only am I reading more effectively and rapidly, but I am also exploring new reading materials which I have previously shunned, such as newspapers, magazines, and novels. To my surprise, I find myself eagerly awaiting a chance to browse through a bookstore, or to sneak a glimpse at the day's news in between classes. What a wealth of knowledge I had gained through an enjoyable pastime.

School has really broadened my horizons. It seems as if lately most of my free time has been spent in reading; not only am I reading more effectively and rapidly, but I am also exploring new reading materials which I have previously shunned, such as newspapers, magazines, and novels. To my surprise, I find myself eagerly awaiting a chance to browse through a bookstore, or to sneak a glimpse at the day's news in between classes. What a wealth of knowledge I have gained through an enjoyable pastime.

In the past five frames, you have been working with verb problems of two kinds: (1) meaning problems, which come up when you aren't sure of how to express a certain time relationship correctly; and (2) form problems, which come up when you aren't sure what the correct form of the verb is. Meaning problems can be solved by paying careful attention to the time element in what you write and by observing how other writers use verb tenses. Form problems can be solved by studying lists like those in grammar books and by noticing unusual past and perfect forms whenever you see them. If you don't know the right forms of a verb, look them up. Everybody forgets verb forms once in a while.

Part 3
Singular and Plural

Forming plurals is basically a matter of spelling. However, there are some guides we can give you to help you in writing plurals.

This segment of the book explains these spelling tips and gives examples of each one. When you finish this part of the book, you will be able to form the plural of the words you will probably be using most often in your writing.

230

Compare the following columns of words:

A	*B*
I	we
one	many
book	books
man	men
he	they

What is the common differences between the words in column *A* and the words in column *B*?

____

____

(*Your own words*)

The words in column *A* are singular (refer to only *one* thing or person); the words in column *B* are plural (refer to *more* than one thing or person).

231

Singular nouns are words that refer to a single person or thing. *Plural nouns* are words that refer to *more than one* person or thing. In the English language, most plural nouns are formed by adding *-s* to the singular.

The plural of each of the following singular nouns is formed by adding *-s.* Fill in the blanks in column *B* with the plural form of the words in column *A.*

	A		*B*
1.	one drink	two	______
2.	one cigarette	three	______
3.	one thought	four	______
4.	one guitar	five	______

1. drinks
2. cigarettes
3. thoughts
4. guitars

232

Examine the following singular and plural nouns:

SINGULAR	*PLURAL*
class	classes
ash	ashes
watch	watches
kiss	kisses

How do words ending in *-sh, -ch,* and *-ss* form their plurals?

____

by adding *-es*

233

There are several other patterns (besides adding *-s* or *-es*) for changing singular nouns to plural nouns.

If a word ends in *-y,* and is preceded by a consonant, change the *y* to *i* and add *-es.* Look at the following examples:

SINGULAR	*PLURAL*
family	families
library	libraries

If a words ends in *-y,* and is preceded by a vowel, add an *-s* to the word to form the plural:

SINGULAR	*PLURAL*
boy	boys
tray	trays

Form the plural of the following words:

baby
donkey
buoy
buddy

babies
donkeys
buoys
buddies

234

Some words do not follow any rules in forming plurals. Look at the following examples.

SINGULAR	*PLURAL*
woman	women
child	children
leaf	leaves
sheep	sheep

If you are unsure of the plural of a particular word, look it up in the dictionary.

Suppose you are writing a paper. You are not sure of the plural of the word "calf" and look it up in the dictionary. The dictionary says "calf, *n.* (*pl.* calves)."

What is the plural of "calf"?

---

calves

235

Now, we'll look at the plurals of *pronouns.* Like nouns, pronouns refer to persons or things—but without naming them.

It is generally easy to see which pronouns are singular and which are plural. The only one that might be confusing is the pronoun "you." In some cases it is singular and in some cases it is plural, depending on the way it's used.

Examine these two sentences:

a. I want to see *you* alone after class.
b. If *you* all come over later, we can have a party.

1. Which sentence, if any, uses the *singular* pronoun "you"?

   Answer ________
   (*a*) or (*b*)

2. Which sentence, if any, uses the *plural* pronoun "you"?

   Answer ________
   (*a*) or (*b*)

1. *a*
2. *b*

236

Column *A* contains a list of nouns. Some are singular and some are plural. Match each of these nouns with the correct singular or plural pronoun from column *B*.

For example: __*c*__ John
__*g*__ John and Mary
__*f*__ John and I

	A	*B*
______	1. the actor	*a.* I
______	2. Steve and Joe	*b.* you
______	3. the waitress	*c.* he
______	4. the waitresses	*d.* she
______	5. you students	*e.* it
______	6. the book	*f.* we
______	7. the elephants	*g.* they
______	8. the driver and I	

1. *c*
2. *g*
3. *d*
4. *g*
5. *b*
6. *e*
7. *g*
8. *f*

In the next few frames, we'll use what you've learned about verbs, nouns, and pronouns to solve another writing problem.

When the subject of a sentence is a *singular* noun or pronoun, the *verb* in that sentence must be singular too. When the subject is plural, the verb must be plural. When these rules are broken, we say the subject and verb don't *agree.*

237

Almost every language in the world has rules about subject and verb *agreement.* In most languages—including English—the basic rule is that a singular subject requires a ________________ verb form and a plural subject requires a ________________ verb form.

singular
plural

238

You have learned how to recognize singular and plural nouns and pronouns. Now look at the following examples of verb forms used with each:

SINGULAR	*PLURAL*
I stand	we stand
that man stands	those men stand
he stands	they stand
you stand	you stand
that woman stands	
she stands	

What *two forms* of the verb "stand" can you find in these columns?

1. ________________

2. ________________

(*Either order*)

1. stand
2. stands

239

Of the two forms, "stand" and "stands," which did you find only in the singular column? (*Look back at the last frame to answer this question.*)

____

stands

240

The "stands" form is always singular. Which of the following, according to frame 238, applies to the "stand" form? (*Check the correct answer.*)

______ *a.* It is always singular.
______ *b.* It is always plural.
______ *c.* It can be singular or plural.

c

241

"Stands" is a *singular* verb form. Almost all singular nouns and pronouns would require "stands" instead of "stand."

Look at these examples and then answer the question below.

I stand.
A man stands.
He stands.
You (singular) stand.
The book stands.
It stands.
The woman stands.
She stands.

Which two singular subjects do *not* use "stands"?

________________ and ________________

(*Either order*)

I
You

242

When any singular noun or pronoun (except "I" and "You") is the subject of a clause, the letter ______ must be added to the simple form of the verb.

-s

243
For some verbs with singular subjects, it is necessary to add *-es* instead of *-s*.

Examine the following verb forms: he *catches*, she *watches*, it *washes*, the child *wishes*, the quarterback *passes*, the dog *messes*.

From the above, you can conclude that *-es* instead of *-s* must be added to verbs ending in ______ , ______ , or ______ when used with a singular subject.

(Any order)

-sh
-ch
-ss

244
Now examine the following sentences:

1. *a.* I *carry*.
   b. He *carries*.
2. *a.* I *worry*.
   b. He *worries*.

In each of these cases, what changes were made in the original verb so that it would agree with the subject "He"?

____

(Your own words)

y was changed to *i* before *-es* was added.

245
Correct the following verbs so that they agree with their subjects.

1. He *play* on the school's football team.

   ____

2. She *patch* her jeans when they tear.

   ____

3. She *dress* in the latest fashion.

   ____

4. He *hurry* to the phone as soon as it rings.

   ____

1. plays
2. patches
3. dresses

(If you missed any of these three, review frame 243.)

4. hurries

(If you missed this one, review frame 244.)

246

With *all plural* subjects—plus "I" and "you," singular—you should *not* add *-s* or *-es* to the verb.

For each of the following subjects, write the correct form of the verb "wait." (*Write the correct verb for each subject in the blanks.*)

a. I ______________________________
b. the nurse ______________________________
c. the women ______________________________
d. you (singular) ______________________________
e. you (plural) ______________________________
f. the universe ______________________________

a. I wait
b. the nurse waits
c. the women wait
d. you (singular) wait
e. you (plural) wait
f. the universe waits

247

In the following sentences, decide which verb form is required for the subject and verb to agree. (*Write the correct verb in the blank.*)

1. I ____________________ for him every day at four.
   (watch) (watches)

2. A dog quickly ____________________ who its master is.
   (learn) (learns)

3. The party ____________________ just at the stroke of midnight.
   (begin (begins)

4. They all _______________ to hear the concert.
(want) (wants)

5. We _______________ a film in Sociology class every Friday.
(see) (sees)

6. It _______________ a lot of effort to stay awake in Math class.
(take) (takes)

7. You _______________ us that same joke evey time.
(tell) (tells)

1. watch
2. learns
3. begins
4. want
5. see
6. take
7. tell

248

Now let's see if you can recognize where changes must be made in a verb form to make it agree with its subject. Read the following sentences. Then rewrite only the *incorrect* sentences so that they are correct (so that the subjects and verbs agree). If the sentences are correct, no answer is required.

1. We *make* better time on the turnpike.

____

2. He *make* more money than his wife *do.*

____

3. They *are* both actors.

____

4. She *are* married now.

____

5. It *take* an idiot to fail her exams.

____

2. He *makes* more money than his wife *does.*
4. She *is* married now.
5. It *takes* an idiot to fail her exams.

249

You may have noticed that all our examples of changing verb forms have been in the *present tense.* Let's go on now and see what happens in the two other verb tenses we have learned.

Take the past tense of stand (stood). Examine the following subjects and verbs:

I stood	you stood
you stood	they stood
he stood	the men stood
the man stood	we stood

Note that some of the subjects are singular and some are plural. Is there any change in the verb?

Answer ____________
(yes) (no)

no

250

In the *simple* past tense, *no changes* are necessary in the verb form to make the subjects agree.

Write the correct forms of the *past* tense of the verb "want" in the blanks next to the subjects below. (The past tense of "want" is "wanted.")

1. I ____________
2. you (singular) ____________
3. he ____________
4. she ____________
5. it ____________
6. we ____________
7. you (plural) ____________
8. they ____________

1. wanted	5. wanted
2. wanted	6. wanted
3. wanted	7. wanted
4. wanted	8. wanted

251

No changes are necessary in the simple ______________ tense of a verb in
(present) (past)

order for the subject and verb to agree.

past

252

Using the verb "want," complete the following sentences in the tense indicated in parentheses.

1. Allen ______________ to see her. (*present*)
2. Allen ______________ to see her. (*past*)

1. wants
2. wanted

253

Now examine these examples of the *future* tense.

I will forgive
you will forgive
he will forgive
she will forgive
we will forgive
they will forgive

1. Does the main verb ("forgive") *change* as the subjects vary between singular and plural?

   Answer ____________
   (yes) (no)

2. Does "will" change as the subjects vary?

   Answer ____________
   (yes) (no)

1. no
2. no

254

The simple future tense, then, uses only one verb form that agrees with both singular and plural subjects.

Fill in the future tense of the verb "see" in the following blanks so that the subjects and verbs agree.

1. I ______________
2. you ______________
3. he ______________
4. we ______________
5. you ______________
6. they ______________

1. I will see
2. you will see
3. he will see
4. we will see
5. you will see
6. they will see

255

In the simple future tense, the verb form ______________ change as the
(does) (does not)

subject varies between singular and plural.

does not

256

1. What are the two verb tenses in which the verb forms do *not* change as the subject varies between singular and plural?

   ____

2. In which verb tense *does* the verb form change in order to maintain subject-verb agreement?

   ____

1. future, past
2. present

Most common mistakes that students make concerning subject-verb agreement happen because the students don't know how to *apply* the rules in certain tricky situations.

Let's look at some of these situations.

257

We know that subjects and verbs are used to answer the question:

subject	*verb*
Who (or what)	does what?

You should keep this in mind, especially when you are writing a *question*.

When a sentence is in *question* form, it is often difficult to recognize the subject—since the word order in questions is the *reverse* of the word order in statements.

Which words in the following questions answer the question who (or what)? (*Circle the subject of each sentence.*)

1. Where is the concert?

   (The concert is where?)

2. Do you see the problem here?

   (You do see the problem here?)

3. Are those cars ready to race yet?

   (Those cars are ready to race yet?)

4. Where are the tickets being sold?

   (The tickets are being sold where?)

1. concert
2. you
3. cars
4. tickets

258

What is wrong with this sentence?

Where is the new albums?

____

____

The subject ("albums") is *plural* and the verb ("is") is *singular*.

259

Rewrite this question so that the subject and the verb *agree*.

____

Where are the new albums?

260

We've said that the subject of a question is sometimes difficult to pick out because of the reverse word order. Certain types of statements also have reverse word order. For example:

1. Here comes the blushing bride.
2. There goes the frightened groom.
3. Here are five rules to follow.

Circle the subject in each of the above sentences.

1. (bride)
2. (groom)
3. (rules)

261

As you may have guessed, the words "where," "there," "here," and "when" can *never* be the subject of a clause.

1. Is the following a sentence?

   There are.

   Answer ____________
   (yes) (no)

2. Explain your answer.

   ____

1. no
2. There is no subject. *or* "There" can never be a subject.

262

Is the following as sentence? (Is it a complete question?)

Where are?

Answer ____________
(yes) (no)

no
(There is no subject in "Where are?")

263

Rewrite all these sentences so that they are correct, by correcting the verbs.

1. Where is the mistakes in your paper?

____

2. Here is the ones ready for action.

____

3. Does you know her or not?

____

4. There go my boyfriend with another woman.

____

5. Are the pub open?

____

6. When is you going camping?

____

1. Where *are* the mistakes in your paper?
2. Here *are* the ones ready for action.
3. *Do* you know her or not?
4. There *goes* my boyfriend with another woman.
5. *Is* the pub open?
6. When *are* you going camping?

264

In the following paragraph, some of the subjects and verbs do not agree. Circle the *verbs* that are incorrect, and write them correctly in the blanks below.

> Success is sometimes hard to measure. Suppose one of your jobs is to create signs that keeps house trailers from being set up on a piece of property for six months. Immediately there is an earthquake. A huge hole appear in the ground, and after 6 months there is still no house trailers on the property. Were it your signs that kept them away, or was it the earthquake?

(keeps)	keep
(appear)	appears
(is)	are
(Were)	Was

265

In writing, the word "each" often leads to errors in subject-verb agreement. Look at this example:

> Each of the strikers carries a picket sign.

The correct verb in this sentence is "carries."

The subject is ________________ .
(Each) (strikers)

Each

266

The word "Each refers to ____________________ person or thing.
(one) (more than one)

one

267

What form of the verb "want" should be used in this sentence? (*Underline the correct answer.*)

Each of our friends (want/wants) to come to our party.

wants

268

The subject "Each" is the signal for a ________________ verb.
(singular) (plural)

singular

269

Here is an example of the same kind of problem:

One of his many worries *is* his weight.

"Is" is the correct verb in this sentence. The subject is ________________ .
(One) (worries)

One

270

Write the correct verb in each of the following sentences.

1. One of us ____________ to be there at five o'clock.
(have) (has)
2. One of the men __________ writing a novel.
(are) (is)
3. Each of those plants ________________ from Australia.
(come) (comes)
4. One of their problems __________ financial.
(are) (is)

1. has
2. is
3. comes
4. is

271

Now look at these examples:

Both the men are cops.
Both our stereos are broken.
All the students want better courses.
All of us are students.

1. What is the subject of the first two sentences? ______________
2. The second two sentences? ______________

1. both
2. all

272

The word "both" always refers to two things. When "both" is used as the subject of a sentence, you know that the verb must be ______________ .
(singular) (plural)

plural

273

The word "all" can be used as the subject of a sentence in one of two ways.

Compare these two sentences:

a. All the house is clean now.
b. All the houses are sold now.

1. In sentence *a*, the subject *all* is ______________ .
(singular) (plural)

2. In sentence *b*, the subject *all* is ______________ .
(singular) (plural)

1. singular
2. plural

274

In the following sentences, the words that "All" refers to are *singular.* Write the correct verbs in the blanks.

1. All my money ___________ gone.
(is) (are)

2. All his hair ___________ falling out.
(is) (are)

1. is
2. is

275

In the following sentences, the words that "All" refers to are *plural.* Write the correct verbs in the blanks.

1. All her clothes ___________ old.
(is) (are)

2. All their grades ___________ been released.
(has) (have)

1. are
2. have

276

In the following sentences *choose* the correct verbs and write them in the blanks.

1. All her friends ___________ going.
(is) (are)

2. All their pets ___________ sick.
(is) (are)

3. All our effort ___________ wasted.
(was) (were)

4. All her term paper ___________ completed.
(is) (are)

1. are
2. are
3. was
4. is

277

Rewrite the following sentences so that they are correct.

1. All our friends is coming.

____

2. All our money were stolen.

____

1. All our friends are coming.
2. All our money was stolen.

278

Two other words that frequently cause trouble when they are used as subjects are "anybody" and "everybody."

Read the following sentences:

Anybody is welcome.
Everybody is entitled to his own opinion.

"Anybody" and "everybody" are signals for a _______________ verb.
(singular) (plural)

singular

279

Rewrite the following sentences so that they are correct:

1. Anybody here are my friend.

____

2. Everybody deserve a chance to attend college.

____

1. Anybody here *is* my friend.
2. Everybody *deserves* a chance to attend college.

280

Once you remember to use singular verbs in sentences to refer to "anybody" and "everybody," you should also remember to use singular *pronouns.*

Read this correct sentence:

Everybody deserves a chance to attend the college of his choice.

What is the pronoun in this sentence that *refers* to the subject "everybody"?

____

his

281

Which of the following sentences is *correct*?

a. Everybody wants his own place.
b. Everybody wants their own place.

Answer ____________
(*a*) or (*b*)

a

282

"His" is a singular pronoun; "their" is a plural pronoun. In the blanks in the following sentences, write the pronouns that are correct.

1. Anybody is entitled to ____________ opinion.
(her) (their)

2. Anybody can bring ____________ guests to the party.
(his) (their)

3. Everybody makes ____________ own mistakes.
(her) (their)

4. Everybody should decide for ____________ .
(himself) (themselves)

1. her
2. his
3. her
4. himself

283

Rewrite the following sentences so that they are correct.

1. Everybody said that their picture was best.

____

2. Anybody who wants to can express their idea.

____

1. Everybody said that *his* (or *her*) picture was best.
2. Anybody who wants to can express *his* (or *her*) idea.

284

When "everybody" or "anybody" is used as the subject of a sentence, all verbs and pronouns that refer to the subject must be ____________________ .
(singular) (plural)

singular

285

Another confusing situation is illustrated by the following examples:

Either Brown or Jones *is* a good English teacher.
Neither he nor his dog *was* anywhere in sight.

When two singular subjects are connected by "or" or "nor," the verb must be ____________________ .
(singular) (plural)

singular

286

Write the correct verb for each of the following sentences:

1. Either she or her mother ______________ there every day.
(sit) (sits)

2. Neither his friend nor his enemy ______________ anything good to say about him.
(have) (has)

3. Either the trainer or the owner ______________ at the track now.
(are) (is)

4. Neither the husband nor his wife ______________ willing to give in to a divorce.
(were) (was)

1. sits
2. has
3. is
4. was

287

Now look at the following examples of subjects joined by "or" or "nor":

> Either the teacher or his assistants will instruct the class.
> Neither the teacher nor his students were at all surprised at the administration's decision.

When one singular and one plural subject are joined by "or" or "nor," the *plural* subject is written ______________ and the verb is ______________ .
(first) (second) (singular) (plural

second
plural

288

Write the correct verb for each of the following sentences:

1. Either she or her friends always ______________ to work.
(drive) (drives)

2. Neither my work nor my grades ______________ ever been good.
(have) (has)

1. drive
2. have

289

When you write, you will have to be able to spot and correct the mistakes you make in subject and verb agreement.

Read through the following paragraph and circle the verbs or pronouns that do not agree with the subjects they refer to.

> Sex are probably a multibillion dollar business. Just think of all the people who make money from man's lust. There is pornographic magazines and movies to arouse you, manuals to instruct you, various devices to aid you, prostitutes to satisfy you, motels to accommodate you, and even special doctors to treat you if something goes wrong. Yes, capitalism have even reached man's most basic desire. Millions is becoming rich on something which was once a private affair between two people.

are

is

have

is

290

Rewrite the paragraph in the previous frame so that it is correct.

____

____

____

____

____

____

Sex is probably a multibillion dollar business. Just think of all the people who make money off man's lust. There are pornographic magazines and movies to arouse you, manuals to instruct you, various devices to aid you, prostitutes to satisfy you, motels to accommodate you, and even special doctors to treat you if something goes wrong. Yes, capitalism has even reached man's most basic desire. Millions are becoming rich on something which was once a private affair between two people.

291

Now write your own paragraph; discuss how you spend your free time in between classes. Have your instructor review the paragraph with you. Pay careful attention to subject–verb agreement.

____

____

____

____

____

Part 4 Adjectives and Adverbs

Descriptive words add more detail to our writing and often make it more interesting. Knowing how to use descriptive words can make ordinary sentences sound more exciting.

When you finish this segment, you will be able to tell when to use *adjectives* and when to use *adverbs* as descriptive words. You will be able to avoid confusing certain adjectives and adverbs (like "real" and "very") which are often used incorrectly.

292

Now we'll go on to describe other "functions" that a word can have in a sentence besides subject, verb, and object.

Look at the following sentences:

The worried husband couldn't sleep.
The husband is worried.

What function does the word "worried" have in *both* sentences?

It describes the husband.

293

The function of the word "worried" in the previous frame does not depend on its position in the sentence, but on the fact that it describes the noun "husband."

In the following examples, circle the words that *describe* the nouns.

1. a suspicious wife
2. the black dress
3. blue skies
4. the doctor looks exhausted
5. Allen is thoughtful

1. suspicious
2. black
3. blue
4. exhausted
5. thoughtful

294

The description words that you just circled are called *adjectives.* Adjectives can also describe pronouns.

Circle the adjectives in the following sentences:

He is too nervous.

They are not friendly.

Are you tired?

nervous

friendly

tired

295

Now examine the italicized words in the following columns:

A	B
We thought of a *quick* answer.	They answered *quickly.*
George is a *heavy* drinker.	He drinks *heavily.*
Is he a *good* runner?	The team runs *well.*
He is *angry.*	He speaks *angrily.*
She is *busy.*	She works *busily.*

1. The italicized words in column *A* describe *nouns* or *pronouns.* The italicized words in column *B* describe ________________ .
2. You can see that there is a common ending for most of the italicized words in column *B.* The common ending is ______ .
3. Look at the *third* sentence in both columns. Instead of changing from "good" to "goodly," the italicized word changes from "good" to ________________ .

1. verbs
2. -ly
3. well

296

Words that describe verbs are called adverbs.

1. The italicized words in column *A* in the previous frame are
   ______________________ .
   (adjectives) (adverbs)
2. The italicized words in column *B* in the previous frame are
   ______________________ .
   (adjectives) (adverbs)

1. adjectives
2. adverbs

297

Because both are modifying words, people sometimes confuse when to use adjectives, which modify nouns and pronouns, and when to use adverbs, which modify verbs, adjectives, or other adverbs. For example, the adjective "real" is often confused with the adverb "really," which means "very." Look at the following sentences.

1. The story that he told is *real*. (Adjective modifying the noun, story)
2. The story that he told is *really* good. (Adverb modifying the adjective, good)

"Real" is an ______________________ .
(adjective) (adverb)

"Really" is an ______________________ .
(adjective) (adverb)

adjective
adverb

Explain the error in this sentence.

That drummer is real good.

____

____

(*your own words*)

"Real," an adjective, is used where "very," an adverb, should be used.

298

Which of the following sentences is correct?

_______ *a.* We are real sorry.
_______ *b.* We are very sorry.

b

The adverb in the sentences above describes the degree to which "We" are sorry.

Which of the underlined words is an adverb?

His problems are real, not imaginary.
He is really worried.

Answer _______________ .
(real) (really)

really

299

In each of the following sentences, write the correct word.

1. There is a _______________ serious problem here.
(real) (very)
2. Is this jacket _______________ made of leather?
(real) (really)
3. You are _______________ helpful to me.
(real) (really)
4. You are _______________ helpful to me.
(real) (very)

1. very
2. really
3. really
4. very

300

Choose the correct modifier in the following and explain why it is the correct choice.

He thinks _______________ .
(careful) (carefully)

"Careful" is an adjective (describes a noun). In this sentence, "He thinks carefully," carefully is being used as an adverb (to describe a verb).

301

In addition to describing verbs, adverbs may also describe adjectives. For example, look at these three sentences:

1. He is not nervous.
2. He is fairly nervous.
3. He is very nervous.

Adverbs are used in these sentences to describe the adjective "nervous." What are the adverbs in these sentences?

1. _______________
2. _______________
3. _______________

1. not
2. fairly
3. very

302

Circle the adjectives and adverbs in the following paragraphs, then complete the story. When you are finished, check your work, then review what you have done with your instructor.

> Leathery-skinned women chattered idly as their half-naked children scampered about in the blazing sun. A heavy stillness of anxiety and despair sneered at their innocent gaiety and slowly tortured their youthful laughter until it forced them to submit to the painful apathy which was so characteristic of their now emotionally barren land. Even the rhythmic sway and the stately picture of the graceful, dark-skinned women as they bore their cherished goods to market was degraded by the persistent threat of injury.

The thought of "doomsday" constantly haunted the inner souls of these people; yet when it came, the bursting flashes of exploding bombs in all their horrible splendor recreated the familiar chaos. The old feelings of anguish and helplessness became new again; people screamed and raced about in fright. Old men were pushed aside as the more agile scooped up children and hurried about, but with nowhere to go. Confused, alone, and fixated in fright, a sole person searched for a familiar face only to be trampled to the ground as the masses swarmed over her. Dazed and horrified, she at first wasn't aware of ______________________________

____

____

____

____

____

____

____

____

____

____

____

303

Adjectives and adverbs can also be used to show comparison. Circle the word used as an adjective in this phrase:

a dirty cloth

304

Suppose you took the dirty cloth in the previous frame and wiped the floor with it. The cloth would then be: (*Check the correct answer.*)

______ *a.* less dirty
______ *b.* dirtier
______ *c.* clean

dirtier

305

At first, the cloth was "dirty." After you wiped the floor with it, it was "dirtier."

When you are using a single adjective as a means of *comparing* two things, its form changes.

The adjective ________________ implies a comparison between two things.
(dirty) (dirtier)

dirtier

306

In the following sentences, *circle* the *adjectives* that imply comparison of two things.

1. She is prettier than his previous girlfriend.
2. This assignment is harder than the last one he gave us.
3. They have decided that they need a bigger apartment.

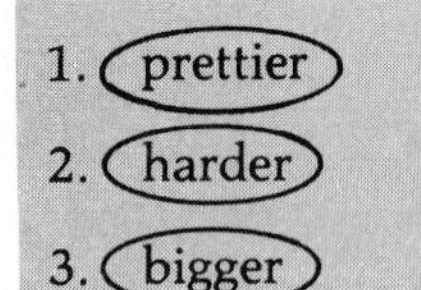

307

Read through the two columns of adjectives below.

hard	harder
tight	tighter
rich	richer
yellow	yellower

Most adjectives change their form by adding ________________ when they are used to express comparison.

-er

308

In the following sentences, write the correct form of the adjective in parentheses.

1. He was much (tall) ________________ than when I saw him last.
2. The music was (loud) ________________ than usual.
3. He can run (fast) ________________ than I.

1. taller
2. louder
3. faster

309

In changing adjectives to the comparative form by adding an *-er* sound, there may be spelling problems.

For example, read through these sets of adjectives: big/bigger, thin/thinner, wide/wider, pretty/prettier, safe/safer.

The next few frames will briefly review some of these spelling problems.

no answer required

Look at these sets of adjectives:

friendly/friendlier, phony/phonier, witty/wittier

From the above, you can conclude that adjectives ending in *-y* are changed to the comparative form by

____

(*Your own words*)

changing *-y* to *-i* and adding *-er, or* dropping *-y* and adding *-ier.*

310

Using adjective forms that express *comparison,* rewrite the sentences below using the adjectives in parentheses.

1. He is (friendly) ________________ than we thought.

   ____

2. They are even (phony) ________________ than he believed.

   ____

3. The cook's work is (easy) ________________ than anyone else's.

   ____

1. He is *friendlier* than we thought.
2. They are even *phonier* than he believed.
3. The cook's work is *easier* than anyone else's.

311

Some adjectives double their last letter and then add *-er.* Examples of these include "thin," "fat," and "big."

Rewrite the following sentences using the correct forms of the adjectives in parentheses to express comparison.

1. She is getting much (thin) ________________ due to poor nutrition.
2. He is (big) ________________ than I thought.

1. She is getting much *thinner* due to poor nutrition.
2. He is *bigger* than I thought.

312

Where an adjective already ends in *-e,* you need only add *-r* to express comparison.

Rewrite the following sentences using the correct forms of the adjectives in parentheses to express comparison.

1. The teacher is much (nice) ________________ outside of the classroom.
2. There couldn't be a (strange) ________________ story than that.

1. The teacher is much *nicer* outside of the classroom.
2. There couldn't be a *stranger* story than that.

313

Most of the adjectives we have used so far have been very short. For longer adjectives, comparison should be expressed by writing *more* in front of the adjective *instead of* adding *-er.*

Which of the following forms do you think is correct?

a. intelligenter
b. more intelligent

Answer ____________
(*a*) or (*b*)

b

314

Which of the following forms are *correct*? (*Check all that apply.*)

_______ *a.* frequenter
_______ *b.* more frequent
_______ *c.* shorter
_______ *d.* more short
_______ *e.* fascinatinger
_______ *f.* more fascinating

b, c, f

315

Adding "more" before an adjective is a simple way to express comparison, but many people make a very common mistake with this method.

One is these adjectives is incorrect. Which? (*Check the incorrect adjective.*)

_______ *a.* tighter
_______ *b.* more interesting
_______ *c.* more busier

c

316

It is incorrect to use *both* "more" and *-er* to express comparison in an adjective. One is enough!

Rewrite "more busier" so that it expresses comparison *correctly*. (*Hint: "busy" is a short adjective.*)

____

busier

317

Rewrite the following sentences so that they are *correct*.

1. Mrs. Hines is more sicker now than ever.

____

2. I have never met a more interestinger person.

____

3. Did you say she was more worrieder or less?

____

1. Mrs. Hines is *sicker* now than ever.
2. I have never met a more *interesting* person.
3. Did you say she was *more worried* or less?

318

The following paragraph contains several mistakes in adjectives that express comparison. Rewrite the paragraph so that it is correct.

> This week was busyer than ever. The more work there was to do, the more interesteder people seem to be in other things. I suppose it is always more simple to make plans that to carry them out.

____

____

____

____

____

This week was *busier* than ever. The more work there was to do, the *more interested* people seemed to be in other things. I suppose it is always *simpler* to make plans than to carry them out.

319

There is another type of comparison that adjectives can express—the comparison of *more than two* things.

The following sentences are examples of this type of comparison.

> Ellen is the *oldest* girl in the family.
> That was the *dullest* movie I've ever seen.
> Mine was the *cheapest* of the three tables.

In using an adjective to compare more than two things, you would add ________________ to the adjective.

-est

320

In the following sentences, write the correct form of the adjectives in parentheses.

1. Kathy is the (smart) ________________ student in the class.
2. He was the (fast) ________________ runner on the team.
3. Their room is the (clean) ________________ in the house.

1. smartest
2. fastest
3. cleanest

321

The *same* spelling rules we discussed earlier apply to adjectives that compare more than two things.

In the following sentences, write the correct form of the adjective in parentheses:

1. He is the (friendly) ________________ person in our class.
2. Of the three old men, my uncle is the (dirty) ________________ .
3. Steve always wants the (easy) ________________ job.

1. friendliest
2. dirtiest
3. easiest

322

In the following sentences, write the correct form of the adjective in parentheses.

1. For two years he was the (thin) ________________ man on the team.
2. That is the (big) ________________ dog I've ever seen!

1. thinnest
2. biggest

323

In the following sentences, write the correct form of the adjective in parentheses:

1. That is the (sure) ________________ way to get caught.
2. She was the (close) ________________ person to the car.
3. His wheels leave the (wide) ________________ tracks of all four cars.

1. surest
2. closest
3. widest

324

The same guideline about *length* also applies to adjectives that express comparison of more than two things. For *longer* adjectives, write *most* in front of the adjective instead of adding *-est.*

Which of the following forms do you think is *correct*?

a. interestingest
b. most interesting

Answer ____________
(*a*) or (*b*)

b

325

Which of the following forms are correct? (*Check all that apply.*)

______ *a.* cleanest
______ *b.* most clean
______ *c.* valuablest
______ *d.* most valuable
______ *e.* richest
______ *f.* most rich

a, d, e

326

When you use "most" with an adjective, you should *not* also add *-est* to the adjective.

Which one of these adjectives is *incorrect*? (*Check the incorrect adjective.*)

______ *a.* widest
______ *b.* most interesting
______ *c.* most expensivest

c

327

It is incorrect to use both "most" and *-est* to express comparison of more than two things.

Rewrite "most expensivest" so that it expresses comparison correctly.

____

most expensive

328

Rewrite the following two sentences so that they are *correct*.

1. Diane was the most beautifulest of the three women.

   ____

   ____

2. They painted their kitchen the most brightest shade of yellow.

   ____

   ____

1. Diane was the *most beautiful* of the three women.
2. They painted their kitchen the *brightest* shade of yellow.

329

The following paragraph contains several mistakes in adjectives that express comparison. Rewrite the paragraph so that it is correct.

> Larry is the competentest employee in the office. I think that is because he is the one interestedest in his work. During his first week, he reorganized our filing system so that it is now the simpleest one in the building. All in all, he is probably the most valuablest person here.

____

____

____

____

____

____

Larry is the *most competent* employee in the office. I think that is because he is the one *most interested* in his work. During his first week, he reorganized our filing system so that it is now the *simplest* one in the building. All in all, he is probably the *most valuable* person here.

330

The following paragraph contains several mistakes in adjectives that express comparison. Rewrite the paragraph so that it is correct.

Denims are the bigger thing in today's fashion industry; they are going everywhere, on everybody, and with good reason. Not only are they more cheaper than most other fabrics, but they are also more comfortable and more easy to care for than more dressy pants. Shopping for jeans is even more easy than shopping for more dressy slacks. There are many shops which sell only jeans, and the selection is usually unbelievable. One can choose from many styles, ranging from the traditionaler, Western style to the moderner, patched jeans. Even colors range from the most bright to the most dull shades, of course, including the all-time favorite blue jean.

____

____

____

____

____

____

____

____

Denims are the *biggest* thing in today's fashion industry; they are going everywhere, on everybody, and with good reason. Not only are they *cheaper* than most other fabrics, but they are also *more comfortable* and *easier* to care for than *dressier* pants. Shopping for jeans is even easier than shopping for *dressier* slacks. There are many shops which sell only jeans, and the selection is usually unbelievable. One can choose from many styles, ranging from the *more traditional,* Western style, to the *more modern,* patched jeans. Even colors range from the *brightest* to the *dullest* shades, of course, including the all-time favorite blue jean.

331

You have learned that adjectives can express comparison. Now we will see how adverbs express comparison. An adverb is a word used to describe an activity or a process rather than a thing (noun). Circle the word used as an adverb in the following sentence.

He held tightly to the windowsill.

tightly

332

When you use an adverb as a way of *comparing* two actions, its form changes.

The adverb "_______________" implies a *comparison* between two
(tightly) (more tightly)
actions.

more tightly

333

In the following sentences, circle the adverbs that express comparison.

1. He thinks more quickly when he's rested.
2. The child ate more eagerly when he realized it was chocolate.
3. She dresses more simply for school than for work.
4. It's impossible to do this job more easily.

1. more quickly
2. more eagerly
3. more simply
4. more easily

334

Adverbs that express comparison almost always use the word "more." The only adverbs that add *-er* are those that can also be used as *adjectives* (for example, *early, close*). These adverbs change their form by adding *-er.*

Write the *correct* form of the adverb in parentheses in the blanks.

1. She arrived (early) _______________ than we expected.
2. Their car was parked (close) _______________ to mine than necessary.
3. Why does he have to work (hard) _______________ than anyone else?

1. earlier (compares the time she *arrived* with the time we expected her to arrive)
2. closer (compares the way they *parked* with the way they should have parked)
3. harder (compares the way he *has to work* with the way anyone else works)

335

In the blanks, write the correct form of the adverbs in parentheses.

1. The class began an hour (early) ______________ than usual.
2. We think he should work (hard) ______________ than he does.
3. He can row (steadily) ______________ since he quit smoking.
4. Steve writes (correctly) ______________ than he used to.

1. earlier
2. harder
3. more steadily
4. more correctly

336

Rewrite the following sentences so that they are *correct.*

1. She thinks logicallier than the teacher.

____

2. Our car was ready more early than he had promised.

____

3. Does it run smoothlier now that it's fixed?

____

1. She thinks *more logically* than the teacher.
2. Our car was ready *earlier* than he had promised.
3. Does it run *more smoothly* now that it's fixed?

337

Just as it is wrong to use *both* "more" and *-er* for comparative adjectives, it's wrong to use both "more" and *-er* for comparative adverbs.

Rewrite the following sentences so that they are correct.

1. We left more later than they did.

____

2. He laughed more louder the second time.

____

1. We left later than they did.
2. He laughed more loudly the second time.

338

Write your own paragraph, comparing and contrasting males and females. Use as many comparative adverbs and adjectives as you can. When you have finished, review your paragraph with your instructor.

____

____

____

____

339

Adverbs can also express comparison of more than two actions. In the following sentences, circle the adverbs that express such a comparison.

1. Of all the students, John writes most clearly.
2. She thinks most quickly when she's under pressure.
3. His department is most often responsible for messing up.

340

Almost all adverbs use "most" to express a comparison of more than two actions. Only those adverbs which keep the same form as adjectives add *-est*.

In the following sentences, write the correct form of the adverbs in parentheses:

1. Of all the secretaries, she leaves (early) ________________ every day.
2. They work (hard) ________________ between 4:30 and 5:00.
3. Of the three of us, his arrow came (close) ________________ .

1. earliest
2. hardest
3. closest

341

In the following sentences, write the correct form of the adverbs in parentheses.

1. Of all our furniture, that chair breaks (often) ________________ .
2. He visits the last of his three ex-wives (frequently) ________________ .
3. Of all the cars I have ever owned, this one runs (dependably) ________________ .

1. most often
2. most frequently
3. most dependably

342

Just as it is incorrect to use "more" and *-er* with the same adverb, it is wrong to use "most" and *-est* with the same adverb.

Rewrite the following sentences so that they are correct.

1. He sees me most oftenest on Sunday.

____

____

2. Of all my family, my sister lives most closest to me.

____

____

1. He sees me *most often* on Sunday.
2. Of all my family, my sister lives *closest* to me.

343

The following paragraph contains several mistakes in adverbs that express comparison. Rewrite the paragraph so that it is correct.

George is most oftenest at the radio station. The show he does frequentliest is the midnight jazz show, but his friends expect him to show up any time of day. He works most hard at the station because jazz is what interests him most.

George is *most often* at the radio station. The show he does *most frequently* is the midnight jazz show, but his friends expect him to show up any time of day. He works *hardest* at the station because jazz is what interests him most.

344

There is a very common mistake that people make when using adjectives and adverbs to express comparison. That mistake is using the *wrong form* of the adjective or adverb for the type of comparison intended. An obvious example would be a sentence like this one:

She is prettiest than her sister.

Rewrite the above sentence so that it is *correct.*

She is *prettier* than her sister.

345

The following sentence is also incorrect, although the structure in this case makes it less obvious:

She is the prettiest of the two girls.

Rewrite this sentence so that it is correct (*without* changing the structure).

____

She is the *prettier* of the two girls.
(Only two girls are being compared here—"she" and some other girl.)

346
Write the correct form of the adjective in the blank below.

Of the three girls, she is the ____________________ .
(prettier) (prettiest)

prettiest

347
Write the correct form of the adjective in the blank below.

Of all these books, which is ________________ interesting?
(more) (most)

most

348
The following sentences deal with both adjectives and adverbs. Write the correct forms for each sentence in the blanks.

1. He listed many reasons, but the last one was ________________ important. (most) (more)
2. Of the two students, I think John studies ____________________ . (harder) (hardest)
3. If we must get three, then we should buy the ____________________ ones in the pile. (cheaper) (cheapest)
4. The parkway is ________________ crowded than the turnpike. (more) (most)

1. most
2. harder
3. cheapest
4. more

349

Rewrite the following sentences so that they are correct.

1. This assignment is the easier one we've had all year.

2. He agreed with us most quickly than his boss did.

3. Of all my classes, math is the more difficult.

4. Of the two papers, yours was most interesting.

1. This assignment is the *easiest* one we've had all year.
2. He agreed with us *more* quickly than his boss did.
3. Of all my classes, math is the *most* difficult.
4. Of the two papers, yours was *more* interesting.

350

The following paragraph contains mistakes in adjectives and adverbs that express comparison. Rewrite the paragraph so that it is correct.

When vacation began, we had to decide which was most important: scenery or speed. We knew we could travel more faster on the superhighways than the back roads, but we were most interested in seeing trees than billboards.

When vacation began, we had to decide which was *more* important: scenery or speed. We knew we could travel *faster* on the superhighways than the back roads, but we were *more* interested in seeing trees than billboards.

351

There is another common mistake people make when they use certain adjectives and adverbs to express comparison. They forget the correct forms of *irregular* adjectives and adverbs that do *not* add "more," *-er,* "most," or *-est.*

Circle the words used as *adjectives* in the following sentences.

He is a good cook.
His wife is a better cook.
His mother is the best cook.

good
better
best

352
Which of the following adjectives express some degree of *comparison*? (*Check all that apply.*)

______ *a.* good
______ *b.* better
______ *c.* best

b, c

353
"Better" and "best" are forms of the adjective ________________ .

good

354
In the following sentences, fill in the blanks with the correct form of the adjective in parentheses.

She is a good swimmer.
Her sister is a (good) ________________ swimmer than she is.
Their father is the (good) ________________ swimmer in the family.

better
best

355

Other irregular adjectives and adverbs that do *not* express comparison by adding *-er* or *-est* are the following:

a. bad, worse, worst
b. far, farther, farthest
c. many, more, most
d. well, better, best

356

In these sentences, write the correct form of the adjective or adverb in parentheses in the blanks.

1. His painting is bad, but hers is (bad) ________________ .
2. The ball he threw went far, but Bill's went (far) ________________ .
3. She did me many favors, but I did her (many) ________________ .
4. Allen did well, but I did (well) ________________ .

1. worse
2. farther
3. more
4. better

357

Sometimes, just out of habit, people add *-er* or *-est* (or "more" or "most") to irregular adjectives and adverbs. Doing this is incorrect, because the forms of these words *already* imply comparison. It's like writing "more busier."

Rewrite the following sentences so that they are correct.

1. His cold is worser today.

   ____

2. I traveled the fartherest of anyone.

   ____

3. That's the goodest excuse I've ever heard.

   ____

4. He believes in getting the mostest out of life.

   ____

5. He shoots pool well, but Greg plays more better.

   ____

1. His cold is *worse* today.
2. I traveled the *farthest* of anyone.
3. That's the *best* excuse I've ever heard.
4. He believes in getting the *most* out of life.
5. He shoots pool well, but Greg plays *better.*

358

The following paragraph contains mistakes in comparing certain adjectives and adverbs. Rewrite the paragraph so that it is correct.

> The senator was the better campaigner I ever saw. I traveled on most speaking tours than most reporters and I never saw a man travel fartherer to win votes. He spoke in the worstest slums and the richest clubs. He may not have been the most best speaker, but he was certainly the most best politician.

____

____

____

____

____

____

____

____

The senator was the *best* campaigner I ever saw. I traveled on *more* speaking tours than most reporters, and I never saw a man travel *farther* to win votes. He spoke in the *worst* slums and the richest clubs. He may not have been the *best* speaker, but he was certainly the *best* politician.

359

So far the comparisons we have been making with adjectives and adverbs have been in the general direction "many," "more," "most"—but it's also possible to go in the other direction.

Our very first example was that of a dirty cloth, which grew "*dirtier*" the more we used it. Now suppose we *washed* the cloth. It would then be: (*Check the correct answer.*)

_______ *a.* dirtier
_______ *b.* dirtiest
_______ *c.* less dirty

c

Fill in the blank in the following sentence.

She has little money, and I have even _______________ money.

less

360
When the adjective "little" is used to mean a *small amount,* the word that indicates an even *smaller* amount is "less."

1. Look at this phrase: "a little boy." Which of the following *comparisons* is correct?

   a. a littler boy
   b. less boy

   Answer ___________
   (*a*) or (*b*)

2. Now look at this phrase: "a little water." Which of the following comparisons is correct?

   a. a littler water
   b. less water

   Answer ___________
   (*a*) or (*b*)

1. *a*
2. *b*

361
When the adjective "little" is used to mean *physical size,* the comparison form is "*littler.*"

When the adjective "little" is used to mean a *small amount,* the comparison form is _______________ .

less

362

Fill in the blanks in the following sentences with a word that means a *smaller amount.*

1. He gave me little help, and his secretary gave me ________________ .
2. Ann had a little money, and after the movie last night she had ________________ .
3. We have even ________________ luck than they do.

1. less
2. less
3. less

363

Now read these sentences:

a. Of all the people I know, she talks the least.
b. He earns the least money of anyone in the office.
c. She contributed the least for the party.

When a form of "little" is used to mean the *smallest amount,* the form used is ________________ .

least

364

Fill in the blanks in the following sentences:

Ann has little luck.
Her sister has ________________ luck.
Of the three of them, their mother has the ________________ luck.

less
least

365

Now read the sentence below:

We have *less* food.
We have *fewer* cans of food.

1. Which of the italicized adjectives refers to a *singular* noun?

   Answer ______________
   (less) (fewer)

2. Which of the italicized adjectives refers to a *plural* noun?

   Answer ______________
   (less) (fewer)

1. less (refers to *food*)
2. fewer (refers to *cans*)

366

To refer to smaller *numbers* (plural) of things, use the adjective "fewer."

To refer to a smaller *amount* (singular) of something, use the adjective "less."

Which adjective should be used in these sentences?

1. I have ________________ hope now than ever.

   Answer ______________
   (less) (fewer)

2. I have ________________ friends now than ever.

   Answer ______________
   (less) (fewer)

1. less
2. fewer

367

Fill in the blanks in the following sentence.

He has ______________ (less) (fewer) money, but I have ______________ (less) (fewer) problems.

less
fewer

368

Rewrite the following sentences, using "less" and "fewer" correctly.

1. There are less courses being offered this semester.

 ____

2. There is fewer beer left than we thought.

 ____

3. There are less reasons to worry.

 ____

4. Our class made less mistakes at the end of the term.

 ____

5. Has there been fewer rain this year?

 ____

1. There are *fewer* courses being offered this semester.
2. There is *less* beer left than we thought.
3. There are *fewer* reasons to worry.
4. Our class made *fewer* mistakes at the end of the term.
5. Has there been *less* rain this year?

369

The following paragraph contains several incorrect adjectives and adverbs. Read through the paragraph and *circle* all the incorrect adjectives and adverbs.

In the earlyest legends, the gods were responsible for human actions. People believed that good spirits tried to make men more good by guiding them, and that bad spirits tried to make men worser by tempting them. The belief that these spirits could also enter a person and make him insane was even most frightening to people than the belief in the spirits' outside influence. Such beliefs are more commoner than you might think, even though less people today believe in spirits.

370

Write the *correct* form of each of the adjectives and adverbs you circled in the previous frame.

1. ______________________________
2. ______________________________
3. ______________________________
4. ______________________________
5. ______________________________
6. ______________________________

1. earliest
2. better
3. worse
4. more frightening
5. more common
6. fewer

In the last section, you learned what mistakes to avoid when you express comparisons with adjectives and adverbs. In the next section, you will learn to use subject and object pronouns carefully.

Part 5 Subject and Object Pronouns

When we write, we sometimes prefer to use pronouns instead of nouns. This part of the book will give you some hints for the use of subject and object pronouns.

371

This segment will also explain the difference between direct and indirect objects and will give you some clues as to how to recognize them.

So far, we know that every sentence must have at least two basic elements—a subject and a verb—to answer the question:

subject	verb
Who (or what)	does what?

Now look at this question:

subject	verb	
Who (or what)	does	whom (or what)?

We learned in Section 1 that the word that answers the question in the third column is called the *direct object.*

In the following sentence, what is the direct object?

She collects antiques.

antiques

372

A sentence must have a subject and a verb. However, it may or may not have a direct object.

Which of the following sentences have direct objects? (*Check all that apply.*)

______ *a.* He loves women.
______ *b.* We are waiting.
______ *c.* Alice saw the movie.
______ *d.* Do you smoke?

a
c

373

There is another kind of object that a sentence may have which is called the *indirect object.* Look at the sentences below to see how the indirect object compares with the direct object.

a.	He	bought	the soda.	
	subject	verb	direct object	
	(who or what)	(does)	(what or whom)	
b.	He	bought	Mary	the soda.
	subject	verb	indirect object	direct object
	(who or what)	(does)	(to whom)	(what or who)

The indirect object tells "to or for whom" something was done. What is the indirect object in the following sentences?

a. Mark bought Debbie a ring.

____

b. The instructor gave us a test.

____

a. Debbie
b. us

374

There is another clue for finding the indirect object in a sentence. The indirect object always comes before the direct object. If there is a word in the sentence which answers the question "to whom," but comes after the direct object, you can make it the indirect object by changing the order of the sentence.

Look at the following sentences:

a.	He	brought	the soda	to Mary.
	(who)	(does)	(what)	(to whom)
b.	He	brought	Mary	the soda.
	(who)	(does)	(to whom)	(what)

Notice that the meaning of the sentence doesn't change when you change the word order in this case. In both instances, Mary answered the question "to whom."

Let's suppose we wanted to replace "Mary" with a pronoun. Look at the following examples:

a. He brought a soda to Mary.
b. He brought a soda to *her.*
c. He brought Mary a soda.
d. He brought *her* a soda.

Notice that in both instances, we used the object form of the pronoun to replace the noun.

Some verbs *never* have direct objects. (For example, it is impossible to "die" anything.)

Which of the following sentences do *not* have direct objects? (*Check all that apply.*)

______ *a.* He died of malnutrition.
______ *b.* We were waiting for you.
______ *c.* She always looks like that.

None of these sentences have direct objects.

375
Now examine the following pairs of sentences that *do* have direct objects.

1. *a.* Parents have children.
   b. Children have parents.

2. *a.* I called her.
   b. She called me.

1. The *subject* in sentence 1*a* ("Parents") becomes the *object* in sentence 1*b* ("parents"). Does the word "parents" change *form* as it changes from subject to direct object?

   Answer ____________
   (yes) (no)

2. The *subject* in sentence 2*a* ("I") becomes the *object* in sentence 2*b* ("me"). Does the word "I" change form as it changes from subject to direct object?

   Answer ____________
   (yes) (no)

1. no
2. yes

376
The word "parents" is a noun. The word "I" is a *pronoun.*

In the examples given in the last frame, you observed that the ____________ changed in form when its function changed from
(noun) (pronoun)

subject to direct object.

pronoun

377
Look again at the two sentences.

a. I called her.
b. She called me.

1. When the pronoun "I" in sentence *a* becomes a direct object in sentence *b*, what new form of the pronoun is used in *b*?

 ____

2. When the pronoun "her" changes from direct object in sentence *a* to subject in sentence *b*, what new form of the pronoun is used in *b*?

 ____

1. me
2. She

378
Now compare these two sentences:

They hated him.
He hated them.

What is the *object form* of:

1. the pronoun "they"?

 ____

2. the pronoun "he"?

 ____

1. them
2. him

379

In the following sentences, make the pronouns in parentheses into direct objects.

1. He loved (I) ______ at one time.
2. Did she find (he) ______ in time?
3. The teacher wanted to test (they) ______ .
4. She was so nasty that I wanted to hit (she) ______ .

1. me
2. him
3. them
4. her

380

Here is a list of subject and object pronouns:

SUBJECT	*OBJECT*
I	me
you	you
he	him
she	her
it	it
we	us
they	them

1. Which two of the above pronouns would not change in form when used as direct objects?

you
it

381

Which of these sentences uses a pronoun *incorrectly*?

a. He gave the book to Mark.
b. Marie gave the book to he.
c. Mark gave he the book.

Answer ________________
(*a*), (*b*), or (*c*)

b—("he" is not the subject of the sentence, so the form used should be "him.")
c—("he" is the indirect object so the form used should be "him.")

382

When *two* pronouns are objects, *both* pronouns should be in the object form. Which of the following is correct?

a. It is between her and me.
b. It is between she and I.
c. It is between her and I.
d. It is between she and me.

Answer ____________________
(*a*), (*b*), (*c*), or (*d*)

a

383

When a pronoun is used as an object, which *form* of the pronoun would you use—the subject form or the object form?

____

the object form

384

In the following sentences write the correct pronoun in each blank.

a. I found ____________ just in time.
(he) (him)

b. It was a long time before I could talk to ____________ .
(he) (him)

c. He sat behind ____________ in Anatomy class.
(I) (me)

d. I finally caught you and ____________ together.
(she) (her)

e. This could only happen to you and ____________ .
(she) (her)

f. Now it's over for you and ____________ .
(I) (me)

a. him
b. him
c. me
d. her
e. her
f. me

385

Rewrite the following sentences so that they are correct.

1. He danced with Dawn and I.

____

2. I love Greg and he.

____

3. My boyfriend sent I a present.

____

1. He danced with Dawn and *me*.
2. I love Greg and *him*.
3. My boyfriend sent *me* a present.

386

Here is a common writing error involving another pronoun—"who" and its object form, "whom."

What, if anything, is wrong with the following sentence?

There is a man who I met yesterday.

____

If you said "who" should be "whom," you're right.

387

"Who" and "whom" usually introduce two types of word groups—questions and dependent clauses. "Whom" is simply the object form of "who."

Like the other pronouns we have studied, the correct form to use in a clause is determined by the *function* of the pronoun (subject or object) in its own clause.

Go to the next frame.

no answer required.

388
Read this sentence:

There goes the woman whom I met yesterday.

In the clause "whom I met yesterday," what *function*—subject or object—does "whom" have?

____

object

389
Look at this example:

There is the husband who beats his wife.

What function does "who" have in its own clause?

____

subject

390
Here is another example:

There is the guy with whom I work.

What function does "whom" have in its own clause? (*Clue: the complete clause is "with whom I work."*)

Answer ______________
(subject) (object)

object

391
Correct any pronoun errors you find in the following sentences. Write the correct pronoun in the blank spaces.

a. There were too many people who you offended. ______________
b. When I saw who was there, I left right away. ______________
c. Did you hire the woman who I sent? ______________
d. Were you among the workers who were laid off? ______________

a. whom
c. whom

392

In the following, circle the pronouns that are incorrect, then rewrite the paragraph in the space provided.

I'm surely not going to take Danny with I to a party anymore. I took he to one last night, and, boy, did him embarrass me! No sooner had we arrived than he began flirting with all the girls. Then when them refused, he began insulting their boyfriends. All night long, he was loud and abusive. Before the party really even got started, I had to carry he out, after apologizing for his behavior and paying for the two beer mugs that were broken over his head!

____

____

____

____

____

____

with (I)
I took (he) to one
did (him) embarrass me
when (them) refused
to carry (he) out

I'm surely not going to take Danny with me to a party anymore. I took him to one last night, and, boy, did he embarrass me! No sooner had we arrived than he began flirting with all the girls. Then when they refused, he began insulting their boyfriends. All night long, he was loud and abusive. Before the party really even got started, I had to carry him out, after apologizing for his behavior and paying for the two beer mugs that were broken over his head!

Part 6
Possession

When you complete this segment, you will be able to avoid making mistakes in words that show possession. More specifically, you will learn to avoid errors in showing possession with singular nouns, plural nouns, and pronouns.

393

In the English language, there are several ways to express *possession.* Of course, the most obvious way is by using phrases like, "the sweater *that belongs to him*" or "the car *that belongs to* their family." These are examples of physical ownership, in which a person owns a thing.

There are other kinds of possession expressed in English grammar: for instance, "the attitude that belongs to him," "the management that belongs to the factory," and so on, in which physical ownership is not really the idea.

Possessive forms cover all these areas in the English language. Which of the following phrases express possession? (*Check all that apply.*)

______ *a.* the building that belongs to our landlord
______ *b.* the cat that belongs to our neighbor
______ *c.* the attitude of his friend

a, b, c

394

There are better ways to express possession than using the phrase "belongs to," since we have seen that it can be both clumsy and misleading.

One example of a shorter way to express possession was the phrase "the attitude of his friend," in the previous frame. However, there is an even shorter way. It involves changing both *word order* and *form.*

Look now at this example: his friend's attitude

The word order has changed from the previous example by putting the word "friend" *before* the word "attitude" instead of *after.*

The *form* has changed by adding ______ to the word "friend."

-'s

395

Change the following examples of possession by changing word order and form in the same way you saw them changed in the previous frame.

1. the cat of our brother

____

2. the belief of his teacher

____

3. the opinion of Ellen

____

4. the horn of the car

____

1. our brother's cat
2. his teacher's belief
3. Ellen's opinion
4. the car's horn

396

Change the following sentence so that it expresses *possession* by using the -'s form. Write the new sentence on the blank provided.

1. That was the boat of my uncle.

____

1. That was my uncle's boat.

397

The mark (') that goes before -s to show possession is called the *apostrophe.* A common mistake that people make is to leave out the apostrophe and add only the -s. Look at the following examples of possession.

1. The company's office is on Lark Street.
2. My friend's idea was the best.
3. The newspaper's manager resigned.

398

All our examples so far have been of *singular* nouns. To show possession in a singular noun, you add -'s. But what about *plural* nouns that already end in -s?

Look at the following examples of plural nouns:

friends
companies
students

Here are their correct *possessive* forms:

friends'
companies'
students'

How is possession shown for plural nouns?

____

(*Your own words*)

An apostrophe is added after the final *-s*.

399

Now read this phrase: the ideas of my friends.

Which of the following is a *correct* short form of this phrase? (*Check the correct answer.*)

_____ *a.* my friend's ideas.
_____ *b.* my friends' ideas.
_____ *c.* my friends ideas.

b

(If you checked (*a*) you forgot that -*'s* forms the possessive of *singular* nouns. If you checked (*c*), you forgot the apostrophe.)

400

Which of the following shows *possession*?

a. books
b. books'

Answer __________
(*a*) or (*b*)

b

401

Which of the following shows possession when added to a plural noun ending in *-s*? (*Check the correct answer.*)

_____ *a.* -'s
_____ *b.* (')
_____ *c.* -s

b

402

Change the following plural nouns so that they show possession.

1. books _____
2. cups _____
3. students _____
4. bosses _____

1. books'
2. cups'
3. students'
4. bosses'

403

Rewrite these sentences so that they are correct.

1. Nobody heard the girls voices.

_____

2. Her parents house is one hundred years old.

_____

3. The voters decision was that they should go home.

_____

1. Nobody heard the girls' voices.
2. Her parents' house is one hundred years old.
3. The voters' decision was that they should go home.

404

Which is the correct possessive form of: (*Check the correct answer.*)

1. Ellen

    _______ *a.* Ellens
    _______ *b.* Ellen's
    _______ *c.* Ellens'

2. teachers

    _______ *a.* teachers
    _______ *b.* teacher's
    _______ *c.* teachers'

1. *b*
2. *c*

405

Some of the following phrases are *singular* nouns and some use *plural* nouns. Change each phrase to the *shorter* possessive form.

1. the paper of George

    ____

2. the job of my father

    ____

3. the job of my parents

    ____

4. the respect of her friends

    ____

5. the policy of the universities

    ____

1. George's paper
2. my father's job
3. my parents' job
4. her friends' respect
5. the universities' policy

406

Rewrite the following sentences so that they are *correct.*

1. His fathers car is in the garage.

   ____

2. Our parent's taxes went up this year.

   ____

3. Carols' boyfriend just called.

   ____

1. His father's car is in the garage.
2. Our parents' taxes went up this year.
3. Carol's boyfriend just called.

407

Some plural nouns *do not* end in *-s.* Such plural nouns show possession just like *singular* nouns.

Look at this plural noun: "children." Which of the following forms shows possession *correctly*? (*Check the correct answer.*)

_______ *a.* children'
_______ *b.* childrens
_______ *c.* childrens'
_______ *d.* children's

d

408

The correct possessive form of *children* is *children's.*

Write the correct possessive form of:

1. men ______________________________
2. women ______________________________

1. men's
2. women's

409

Plural nouns that *do not* end in *-s* show possession by adding

________________.

(-s) (-'s) (-s')

-*'s*

410

Change the following plural nouns to show *possession.*

1. firemen ______________________
2. group ______________________

1. firemen's
2. group's

411

Change the following *plural* nouns to their possessive form.

1. men ______________________
2. babies ______________________
3. women ______________________
4. guards ______________________

1. men's
2. babies'
3. women's
4. guards'

412

Rewrite the following sentences so that they are *correct.*

1. The student's final vote was 48 to 7 against.

   ____

2. The policemens' uniforms were missing.

   ____

1. The students' final vote was 48 to 7 against.
2. The policemen's uniforms were missing.

413

Sometimes, the name of a person, place, or thing has more than one word—for example, "King George the Third." If you want to use such names to show possession, add -*'s* or (')—whichever is necessary—to the *last* word.

Which of the following shows possession *correctly*? (*Check the correct answer.*)

______ *a.* King's George the Third
______ *b.* King George's the Third
______ *c.* King George the Third's
______ *d.* King George the Thirds

c

414
Change the following nouns and names to show *possession.*

1. my mother-in-law ______
2. King Philip the Foolish ______
3. the Hall of Fame ______
4. the Hall of Mirrors ______

1. my mother-in-law's
2. King Philip the Foolish's
3. the Hall of Fame's
4. The Hall of Mirrors'

415
Nouns are not the only words that can be used to show possession.

Read these phrases:

the book that belongs to *me*
the house that belongs to *them*
the suit that belongs to *him*

"Me," "them," and "him" are pronouns. The above phrases show possession by the words "that belong."

416
However, the pronouns "me," "them," and "him" in the phrases you just read are in the *object* form. Pronouns have special forms that show *possession* by themselves.

Now read these phrases:

my book
their house
his suit

Do "my," "their," and "his" show possession?

Answer ____________
(yes) (no)

yes

417
Do we need the phrase "that belongs to"?

Answer ____________
(yes) (no)

no

Now look at the phrases again.

418

my book	the book that belongs to *me*
their house	the house which belongs to *them*
his suit	the suit which belongs to *him*

Rewrite the following phrases using a shorter *form* that shows possession.

1. the horse which belongs to me

____

2. the problem which belongs to them

____

3. the job which belongs to him

____

1. my house
2. their problem
3. his job

419
Here is a list of possessive pronouns:

SINGULAR	*PLURAL*
my, mine	our, ours
your, yours	your, yours
his, her, hers, its	their, theirs

Now read the following phrases:

the car that belongs to *you*	*your* car
the thought that belongs to *her*	*her* thought
the money that belongs to *it*	*its* money
the hammer that belongs to *us*	*our* hammer

Rewrite the following phrases to express possession in a shorter, clearer way.

1. the answer that belongs to you

   ___

2. the room that belongs to her

   ___

3. the garden that belongs to it

   ___

4. the interest that belongs to us

   ___

1. your answer
2. her room
3. its garden
4. our interest

420

In the following sentences, write the *correct* form of the pronoun in the blanks.

1. ______ house is on Second Street.
   (We) (Our)

2. ______ aunt is in town.
   (I) (My)

3. ______ tie is too long.
   (He) (His)

4. ______ biggest problem is schoolwork.
   (She) (Her)

5. ______________ boss is looking for you.
(You) (Your)

6. __________ foundation is crumbling.
(It) (Its)

7. ________________ cartoons are best.
(They) (Their)

1. Our
2. My
3. His
4. Her
5. Your
6. Its
7. Their

421

Probably the most common mistake that people make with possessives is in their spelling of "its," which is frequently misspelled "it's." Maybe you think that since "it's" has an apostrophe ('), it must show possession. But what about words like "don't," "can't," and "didn't"? They have apostrophes and do not show possession. In words like "don't," "can't," and "didn't," the apostrophe is used to stand for letters which are omitted; for example, the "o" in not (do not, don't), (did not, didn't), and the "no" in cannot (can't).

"It's" really means "it is"; it does not show possession at all.

Which of the following sentences is correct?

a. Its a beautiful day.
b. It's a beautiful day.

Answer ____________
(*a*) or (*b*)

b

422

Which of the following sentences is correct?

a. Its engine is the stronger.
b. It's engine is the strongest.

Answer ______________
(*a*) or (*b*)

a

423

Fill in the blanks in the following sentences with the *correct* form of "It."

1. (It) ______________ power is enormous.
2. (It) ______________ new director is Carl.
3. (It) ______________ nice seeing you.
4. (It) ______________ reputation is bad.

1. Its
2. Its
3. It's
4. Its

Section 5
The Paragraph

Perhaps the most important awareness a writer/reader in college can have is that there are four basic patterns of thought that writers use to express their thoughts to their audience. The four patterns are: exposition (explanation), persuasion, narration (time order), and description. These patterns either occur in isolation or in combination with other patterns.

In this section we will focus primarily on exposition and description patterns of paragraph development. Exposition is emphasized because it is central to most nonfiction and academic writing; description is stressed because it is central to most fiction and creative writing. The expository pattern is ordinarily one in which the main idea is stated first, is followed by two or three supporting details, and is concluded with a statement summarizing what has been said. The descriptive pattern uses the senses (sight, sound, smell, taste, touch) and figurative language (not literally true language) to create a mental image for the audience. The main idea may be stated in the first sentence or it may be introduced by the first and other sentences. Frequently, in this pattern, the opening sentence is used for creating a dramatic effect which sets up the main idea of the paragraph.

424

There are many ways of giving people information—for example, hand signals, facial expressions, and signs.

In written English, information is usually conveyed by combining phrases and clauses to form *sentences.* Sentences can then be combined in certain ways to form *paragraphs.*

Below are four units of language which provide information. Which of these four would probably provide the most information?

_______ *a.* the sentence
_______ *b.* the phrase
_______ *c.* the clause
_______ *d.* the paragraph

d

425

It is impossible to make a strict rule about *how* sentences should be combined to make paragraphs. In general, though, the sentences are arranged so that information is developed in three steps:

1. A statement of information—called the *topic sentence*
2. Statements that *develop* (1)
3. If necessary, a *conclusion* to (1) and (2)

From the above steps, you can see that a paragraph generally: (*Check the correct answer.*)

_____ *a.* develops *one* idea or item of information
_____ *b.* doesn't give any information
_____ *c.* makes a single statement

a

426

You may be wondering why a simple *statement* isn't enough. For example, who needs a paragraph to develop the statement "Sacramento is the capital of California"? However, you can probably think of other statements which would need some *explanation* before people could understand them. (Expository Pattern)

Read both of the following statements. Which do you think *could* use some explanation?

a. Albany is the capital of New York State.
b. Albany is the dirtiest city in New York State.

Answer __________
(*a*) or (*b*)

b

427

In the sentence "Albany is the dirtiest city in New York State," you could have continued the paragraph by describing the "dirty" aspects of Albany, for example. Such sentences support and develop the information in your first statement.

Which of the following pairs of sentences would develop the statement "Albany is the dirtiest city in New York State"? (*Check the correct answer.*)

_____ *a*. Buffalo is the second-dirtiest city in New York. Syracuse is the third-dirtiest city in New York.
_____ *b*. Its sanitation department is very efficient. The men are well paid.
_____ *c*. Large factories pour tons of soot into the air every day. The trash is allowed to accumulate in large amounts on the sidewalk.

c.

428

After several such sentences that develop a statement, a *conclusion* may be necessary.

Which of the following sentences could function as a *conclusion* to the paragraph we have been discussing? (*Check the correct answer.*)

_____ *a*. Unless pollution and sanitation laws are more strictly enforced, Albany will remain the dirtiest city in New York.
_____ *b*. Albany is the cleanest city in New York State.
_____ *c*. Albany is also the busiest city in New York State.

a

429

Arrange the three common steps in paragraph writing so that they are in *correct order.*

conclusion, topic sentence, development

1. _______________
2. _______________
3. _______________

1. topic sentence
2. development
3. conclusion

430

The following paragraph follows the same pattern of development that you outlined in the previous frame. Read it through once. Then write out the sentences which have the functions listed below.

Some doctors think that there is a relationship between automobile accidents and suicide. Many accidents happen because the driver has been drinking. Many others occur because of speed or other reckless driving behavior. Drivers could avoid all of these factors if they wanted to. Therefore, many doctors suggest that such "accidents" are really self-destructive behavior on the part of the driver. (Persuasive Pattern)

1. TOPIC SENTENCE

   ____

   ____

2. DEVELOPMENT

   ____

   ____

   ____

   ____

   ____

3. CONCLUSION

   ____

   ____

TOPIC SENTENCE
Some doctors think that there is a relationship between automobile accidents and suicide.

DEVELOPMENT
Many accidents happen because the driver has been drinking.
Many others occur because of speed or other reckless driving behavior.
Drivers could avoid all of these factors if they wanted to.

CONCLUSION
Therefore, many doctors suggest that such "accidents" are really self-destructive behavior on the part of the driver.

431

The following paragraph also follows the same pattern. Read it through and then write out the sentences according to the functions listed below.

> Spelling is difficult for some people to master; for others, it is comparatively easy. One of the problems of well-intentioned teachers is that they insist on providing the confused student with a multitude of rules for helping with spelling problems. This practice usually confuses the student and adds to his anxiety about trying to spell. I became a good speller when a teacher of mine gave me only one rule to remember. She suggested that we notice the difference between the way the word looks when spelled correctly and how we expected the word to look; then we were to make up our own personal rule to remember how to spell it. For example, there is a fancy word for when an academic discipline is broken down into classifications; it is called a paradigm. When I heard the word for the first time, I thought the spelling would be paradime, because that is the way the word is pronounced. Now when I have to spell the word I think, "paradime is paradig+m" and I never miss it. That is a personal rule that makes sense to me. Try making up your own spelling rules along these lines and I think you'll find that you're a much better and more confident speller.

1. TOPIC SENTENCE

___

___

2. DEVELOPMENT

___

___

___

___

___

___

3. CONCLUSION

___

___

432

The two examples above are basically expository in nature. That is, they are designed to explain or inform. Notice the difference in the style and sequence of the following descriptive paragraph. Read it through once and then write out the sentences which have the functions listed below.

> The first thing I felt when the icy wind swept under my thrown-off blanket at about nine o'clock this morning was an incredible wave of nausea. How did I get that way? Oh yes, it was one of those you-don't-have-to-have-a-reason-parties at the campus pub. Originally I had gone in the pub because I felt like celebrating the solid "B" I'd earned on my first college term paper. The tension had been building for four weeks and I was glad that it was over and that I had done so well. I ran into one friendly buyer after another and before I knew it, I was returning the favors . . . I quickly checked my finances, and found that I was down to my last quarter. That meant that I had shot my last twenty dollars for the pleasure of this ultimate hangover! Carefully stepping out of bed, I felt the room swirling around my wracked body, knocking me right back into the semi-security of my bedding. Just as I was in the middle of swearing off demon rum forever, the phone began its unwelcome, nerve-jangling call. I crawled-slithered to the receiver and blurted a semicoherent "uh" at it. What do you know, it was the gorgeous music major I had babbled to for much of the latter part of the evening, wanting to know how I felt. I assured her in my deepest voice that I was just in from my morning jog and meditation. . . .

TOPIC SENTENCE

____

____

DEVELOPMENT

____

____

____

____

____

____

CONCLUSION

____

(Notice the presence of time order in this description.)

The presence of time order (narrative) pattern combined with the descriptive pattern in the story above provides a clear example of how to write and identify (read) effectively in this mode. You merely ask yourself, "what happened first?" "what happened second?"

In the pure (isolated) descriptive pattern, the writer uses his or her senses and or figurative language to convey a vivid mental image to his or her audience. Examples of this kind of writing would be: "The nauseating smell of the garlic on the man's breath threatened to overwhelm me." (senses) "That woman's eyes are like emeralds." (figurative language) (For a thorough treatment of figurative language, consult any standard text on composition or literary terms.)

433

No matter whether you're explaining, describing, narrating, or persuading, the basic structure of your paragraph must clearly show your main idea to your reader. One of the best ways to make certain that your intended main idea is clear to your reader is to outline what you want to say before you write.

The following is a step-by-step illustration of how to outline:

(First-rank heading)	I. Main idea
(Second-rank heading)	A. Major supporting detail 1
(Third-rank heading)	1. Important aspect of supporting detail 1 (more detailed information)
(Third-rank heading)	2. Important aspect of supporting detail 1 (more detailed information)
(Second-rank heading)	B. Major supporting detail 2
(Third-rank heading)	1. Important aspect of supporting detail 2 (more detailed information)
(Third-rank heading)	2. Important aspect of supporting detail 2 (more detailed information)

To make the idea of outlining clearer, study carefully the organization and form of this model of persuasive outlining written by George Feinstein, a professor of English at Pasadena City College.

The Trouble with Television Commercials

Thesis statement: Television commercials are deceptive, irritating, and unoriginal.

I. Most TV commercials are basically dishonest.
   A. They appeal to the emotions.
   B. They make false claims.
      1. Hair sprays create instant beauty.
      2. Soaps remove stains by magic.
      3. "Secret ingredients," such as BS-17, make your yellow teeth whiter than white.

II. Commercials are a basic annoyance.
   A. They interrupt programs too frequently.
   B. The dialogue is glib, smug, and unconvincing.
   C. The emphasis on toilet paper, laxatives, and body sweat is vulgar.

III. The commercials lack originality.
   A. The same skits are shown again and again.
   B. Car and clothing salesmen continue to use the same hard sell.
   C. Family troubles involving coffee, laundry, or bad breath are always solved by a friend in twenty-nine seconds.

a. Does each main heading relate to the thesis statement?
b. Does each subheading help to develop the heading above it?
c. Note the numbering system. The first or main rank of headings is always labeled with Roman numerals I, II, III. The second rank of headings is labeled ________________ .
d. The third rank of headings is labeled ________________ .

a. yes
b. yes
c. A, B
d. 1, 2

434
Notice that headings and subheadings in the model outline come in groups of two or more. For example, if there is a I, there must also be a II. If there is an A, there must also be a ______ . If there is a 1, there must also be a ______ .

B
2

435
Again refer to the model outline.

a. The headings of the second rank (A, B, C) are indented ____________ than the headings of the first rank (I, II, III). (more) (less)

b. The headings of the third rank are indented ____________ than the headings of the second rank (A, B, C). (more) (less)

more
more

To write a well-organized paragraph, first write a short clear thesis statement and then an outline (all topic or all sentences, as your teacher suggests). Arrange the outline in logical order with proper lettering and indentations. Follow your outline and write a unified paragraph. This same outlining procedure will be of help later on in writing unified compositions.

436

Writing the *first sentence* of a paragraph is often the hardest part. You should remember that since the purpose of a paragraph is to *inform* the person who reads it, your first sentence should tell him as clearly as possible what your paragraph will be about.

If you are writing a paragraph about how raisins are *prepared,* for example, a good beginning sentence might be: (*Check the best answer.*)

______ *a.* I like fruit.
______ *b.* There are four steps involved in preparing raisins for packaging.
______ *c.* Raisins have more nutritional value than bananas.

b

437

Suppose you are writing a paragraph about the bad effects of a lack of vitamin C in a person's diet.

Read the "first" sentences below and write the sentence that gives the reader the clearest idea of what your paragraph will say.

Vitamins are necessary to health.
Vitamin C is a kind of vitamin.
Lack of vitamin C can harm a person's health.

Lack of vitamin C can harm a person's health.

438

Read the following paragraph, which lacks a topic sentence. Then, *decide* which of the three sentences below expresses most clearly what the paragraph is about. (*Check the correct answer.*)

> His eyes were bloodshot and teary. His hands shook when he lit a cigarette, and he coughed incessantly. Finally, his wife persuaded him to see a doctor.

______ *a.* Bob had a good job.
______ *b.* Bob didn't look healthy at all.
______ *c.* Bob seemed to be in perfect health.

b

439

Now *rewrite* the paragraph in frame 438 using the correct topic sentence provided.

____

____

____

____

____

____

____

____

Bob didn't look healthy at all. His eyes were bloodshot and teary. His hands shook when he lit a cigarette, and he coughed incessantly. Finally, his wife persuaded him to see a doctor.

440

Let's analyze this paragraph briefly, since it is a good example of the three-step process we outlined earlier.

> Bob didn't look healthy at all. His eyes were bloodshot and teary. His hands shook when he lit a cigarette, and he coughed incessantly. Finally, his wife persuaded him to see a doctor.

What is the *topic sentence* of this paragraph?

____

Bob didn't look healthy at all.

441

The topic sentence of the paragraph in frame 440 provides the reader with a *statement* of the writer's opinion about Bob's appearance.

What sentences provide the reader with evidence to *support* the statement in the topic sentence?

1. ____

2. ____

____

1. His eyes were bloodshot and teary.
2. His hands shook when he lit a cigarette, and he coughed incessantly.

442

Write out the sentence in the paragraph in frame 440 that provides the reader with a *conclusion* to the situation described.

____

Finally, his wife persuaded him to see a doctor.

443

There is a relationship between sentence *structure* and sentence *function*. Look carefully at the topic sentences we have seen so far:

Albany is the dirtiest city in New York State.
There are four steps involved in preparing raisins for packaging.
Lack of vitamin C can harm a person's health.
Bob didn't look healthy at all.

All these sentences are: (*Check the correct answer.*)

______ *a.* simple
______ *b.* compound
______ *c.* complex

a

444

We don't mean to imply that all topic sentences must be short, simple sentences. However, since the basic function of a topic sentence is to state an item of information as clearly and directly as possible, we can conclude that a _______________ sentence structure is often used for topic
(simple) (compound) (complex)
sentences.

simple

445

The following sentence would *not* make a good topic sentence for a paragraph describing your reaction to a book. It contains several phrases which say the same thing: "was so good," "I certainly did enjoy reading it," and so on. You don't need all of them.

Gone with the Wind was so good that I certainly did enjoy reading it very much.

Look at the following sentences, and write out the one that would make a better topic sentence.

a. I enjoyed reading *Gone with the Wind* very much.
b. *Gone with the Wind* was a book which in my opinion I enjoyed reading very much.

I enjoyed reading *Gone with the Wind* very much.

Many students assume that "proper" writing must be full of things like "in my opinion," "as a general rule," "moreover," "as it were," and so on. These and other phrases can be very useful in some situations, but they are *not* good writing if they obscure or hide the point you are trying to make. This is especially important to remember when you are writing a topic sentence, which should be *clear* and *direct.*

446

The following sentences all contain phrases which are not necessary to the meaning of the sentence. Rewrite the sentences and leave out the unnecessary phrases or words.

1. In my opinion, *Witchcraft* is the best movie I've ever seen.

____

2. Dr. Allen is, as it were, waiting for a crisis.

____

3. He is on the track team and moveover also on the swimming team.

____

4. In general, I usually agree with her.

____

1. *Witchcraft* is the best movie I've ever seen.
2. Dr. Allen is waiting for a crisis.
3. He is on the track team and also on the swimming team. *or* He is on the track team and the swimming team.
4. I usually agree with her.

So far, we have talked about topic sentences for sample paragraphs in this book. What about topic sentences for paragraphs that *you* write? The next several frames provide you with techniques for writing your own topic sentences.

447

The *first* thing to decide about any paragraph you write is: "What is the paragraph going to be about?" In answering this question, you should be as specific as possible. For example, it would be too vague to decide simply that your paragraph is going to be about giraffes. A more specific topic might be the eating habits of giraffes, or how you feel about giraffes.

Once you have decided—as specifically as possible—what your paragraph is going to be about, your *second* step is to pick out the *key words* in your subject and build a topic sentence around them.

Suppose you decide that you are going to write a paragraph about the fact that giraffes live only in Africa. What *two key words* should you include in your topic sentence?

_______________ and _______________

(*Either order*)

giraffes
Africa

448

By *key words,* we don't mean words like the subject and verb, which you know are necessary in *all* sentences. We mean the clues that you use to tell your reader as specifically as possible what the paragraph will be about.

In a paragraph explaining that giraffes live in herds, what do you think should be the key words in the topic sentence?

________________ and ________________

(*Either order*)

giraffes
herds

449

In a paragraph about the use of helicopters in controlling traffic, what do you think should be the key words in the topic sentence?

____

at least "helicopters" and "traffic"; possibly "control"

450

In a paragraph describing two basic methods of garbage disposal, what do you think should be the key words in the topic sentence?

____

at least "garbage disposal"; probably "two basic methods" ("ways," "techniques," etc.)

451

Using the *key words* we picked out of the last four frames, write what you think would be clear, direct topic sentences for:

1. a paragraph explaining that giraffes live only in Africa

   ____

2. a paragraph explaining that giraffes live in herds.

   ____

3. a paragraph telling that helicopters can be used to control traffic

   ____

4. a paragraph describing the two methods of garbage disposal

____

Sample answers:

1. *Giraffes* live only in *Africa.*
   Giraffes are found only in *Africa.*
2. *Giraffes* live in *herds.*
   Giraffes are found only in *herds.*
3. *Helicopters* are being used to *control traffic.*
   Traffic control is now being done by *helicopters.*
   Helicopters can *control traffic.*
4. There are two basic methods of *garbage disposal.*

452

In the following paragraph, the topic sentence has been left out. *Read* through the paragraph once to see what it is about. *Decide* what the key words are, and *write* a topic sentence for the paragraph.

____.

My first visit was in the summer of 1964, to see the World's Fair. The second time was in 1966, to see friends. The last time I visited New York was just last month, when I went there to look for a job. Maybe soon I'll be a resident of New York instead of a visitor.

Your sentence should be similar to these:

I have (visited, been to, seen) New York three times.
I have made three visits (trips) to New York.

453

In the following paragraph, the topic sentence has been left out. *Read* through the paragraph once to see what it is about. *Decide* what the key words are, and *write* a topic sentence for the paragraph.

Not many school activities hold my interest. ______________________

____.

I go to meetings of this theater group every day, because it seems to relax me. The group is made up of people who write plays and act them out. Usually, we perform for just ourselves, but sometimes we perform for other audiences.

Your sentence should be similar to one of these:

The theater group is the only one which interests me.
(However,) I do belong to the theater group.
(However,) One that does interest me is the theater group.

454

In the following paragraph, the topic sentence has been left out. Write a topic sentence for the paragraph.

____

______________________________ . When he was only a freshman in high school, he played on the varsity team. Throughout high school, he scored an average of twenty-six points a game. Then he was given a basketball scholarship to college. Now people think that Bob has a good chance of becoming a professional someday.

Bob plays basketball very well.
Bob is a good basketball player.

455

The following paragraph contains no topic sentence. *Read* through the paragraph once. *Decide* what the key words are, and *write* a topic sentence for the paragraph.

____

____

The first step is to cut out a pattern on a flat block of wood. Second, spread printer's ink over the surface of the wood block. Third, press the inked block against a sheet of paper. When the ink has dried on the paper, your woodcut is finished.

Sample answers:

A woodcut is made in this way.
There are three steps involved in making a woodcut.

456
Write a topic sentence for the following paragraph.

____

______________________________ . This is done with an instrument which allows doctors to see a baby while it is still in the mother. Such examinations before birth may eventually decrease the number of children who die in their first year of life.

Sample answers:

Babies can now be examined before they are born.
Doctors can now examine babies before they are born.

457
We have discussed *two steps* that help you in writing a topic sentence for your paragraphs. What are they?

1. ____
2. ____

(*Your own words*)

1. Decide what the paragraph is about.
2. Decide what the *key words* are.

458
Suppose you are writing a paragraph. As a first step toward writing a topic sentence, you have decided that it will be about a new way of controlling cancer. Take the second step, and then write a topic sentence for the paragraph.

____

____

Sample answers:

A new way of controlling cancer has been developed.
There is a new way of controlling cancer.

459

Using the same method you used in the previous frame, write *topic sentences* for the following:

1. a paragraph about how hard it is to keep dogs in an apartment

   ____

2. a paragraph telling that Switzerland does not allow women to vote

   ____

Your sentences should be similar to:

1. It is hard to keep dogs in an apartment.
   or Keeping dogs in an apartment is hard.
2. In Switzerland, women are not allowed to vote.
   or Switzerland does not allow women to vote.

460

Read through the following paragraph.

> Spring recess was the best vacation I have ever had. It rained every single day. Our car broke down three times, and we spent all our money trying to get it fixed. We couldn't afford a place to stay, so we had to sleep in the car. Then, when we finally gave up and tried to hitchhike home, we were arrested.

Is there a logical relationship between the topic sentence and the rest of the paragraph?

Answer ____________
(yes) (no)

no

Unless you have ideas about vacations that are different from those of most people, you probably thought the last paragraph didn't make much sense. This was because you read the topic sentence and expected the development to indicate a *good* vacation, not a bad one.

461

The paragraph in the previous frame is an extreme example of what can happen when the topic sentence *isn't* supported by the rest of the paragraph.

In the following paragraph, one sentence does *not* belong with the topic sentence and the rest of the paragraph. Read through the paragraph once and then *cross out* the sentence that doesn't belong.

Here are the directions to get to my house from yours. You walk two blocks north and then turn right on Adams Street. Walk another two blocks to Third Street. My sister lives at the corner of Adams and Third. Then, turn left on Third Street and walk until you see a dirt road with a yellow house on the corner. That's my house.

You should have crossed out the sentence "My sister lives at the corner of Adams and Third," since it wasn't really a part of the directions.

462

Your paragraphs can be very confusing to people who read them if you aren't careful to see that all of your *sentences* relate to what your *paragraph* is about.

In the following paragraph, *cross out* the sentence that doesn't belong.

One of the greatest responsibilities of the Dieri and Kaitish tribal magicians is to bring rain. The Dieri tribe stages a complicated ritual asking the clouds for rain. The Kaitish tribe believes that the rainbow is the son of the rain and keeps his father from falling down. Fire is another important part of a tribe's life. In both these tribes it is the magician's responsibility to please the rainbow or the clouds and persuade them to let the rain fall.

You should have crossed out the sentence "Fire is another important part of a tribe's life." The paragraph is about rain, not fire.

463

Suppose you begin a paragraph with the following topic sentence:

The best book I read this year was about auto racing.

Which of the following sentences *could* belong in the paragraph? (*Check all that apply.*)

______ *a.* It described the first racing cars ever built.
______ *b.* Another book I read was about horses.
______ *c.* It had the names of all the world's fastest drivers.
______ *d.* I once knew a boy whose father raced cars.

a, c

464

Suppose you begin a paragraph with this topic sentence:

Automobile racing is a dangerous sport.

Some of the sentences below belong in a paragraph with this topic sentence. Some do not. Check the sentences that you *could* use in your paragraph.

______ *a.* Many drivers say that they love the danger.
______ *b.* I like horse racing better.
______ *c.* Each year several drivers are killed in accidents.
______ *d.* Soccer is also dangerous.
______ *e.* Sometimes mechanics are hurt too—when cars crash during races.
______ *f.* Cars are less dependable than horses.
______ *g.* Yet spectators, drivers, and mechanics all enjoy the excitement.

a, c, e, g

(The paragraph is not *about* horse racing, soccer, or the dependability of cars vs. horses.)

465

Fill in the blanks, relating your answers to the topic sentences.

Illustrate the statement, "My left hand is unique."

1. For instance, it has ______________________________.
2. As a second example, it ______________________________.
3. It, in addition, ______________________________.
4. Furthermore, it ______________________________.

(Don't balk. You can always say that you use it to "tittup" with your friends, whereas most people use their right.)

5. And finally, my left hand ______________________________.
6. To summarize, the uniqueness of my left hand stems from ______________, ______________________________, and ______________________________.

466

Develop by factual material. "This room is crowded."

1. It contains ______________ desks and ______________ chairs.
2. Second, there are ______________________________.
3. Also, ______________________________.
4. Moreover, ______________________________.
5. And finally, ______________________________.
6. The combination of these many things indicates ______________________________ ______________________________.

467

Develop by comparison. "All girls (boys) have much in common."

1. First of all, they generally have two eyes.
2. ______________________________.
3. ______________________________.
4. ______________________________.
5. And last, but not least, they all have a ______________________.
6. Basically, all girls (boys) ______________________.

468

Develop by contrast. "Although they are both animals, elephants are unlike seals."

1. The seal, for instance, lives in water, whereas ______________________
   ______________________________.
2. Another difference is ______________________.
3. ______________________________.
4. ______________________________.
5. A last point is ______________________.
6. ______________________________.

469

Define. "The word *grass* has a variety of meanings."

1. One meaning is ______________________.
2. To my parents, however, grass ______________________.
3. A cow ______________________.
4. Yet, my dictionary ______________________.
5. But to me, ______________________.
6. To conclude, ______________________.

How does a writer go about developing an idea? Precisely as you have done in the exercises above. Commit yourself to a position by making a statement and then support the idea. If you were to take any one of the items above, omit the numbers, and then write it all out in sentences, you would have a fair paragraph.

470

In the following paragraph, there are several sentences which don't belong. Read through the paragraph once, then cross out the sentences which don't belong and rewrite the paragraph without those sentences.

His goal in life is to be an excellent potter. He works all day forming graceful vases, bowls, and pitchers out of clay. He spends the rest of his time glazing and baking these pots so that they will be beautiful and durable. His girl friend makes silver jewelry. She is very talented, too. His teachers say that if he continues working at this rate, he will realize his goal very soon.

____

____

____

____

____

____

You should have crossed out the sentences:

His girl friend makes silver jewelry. She is very talented, too.

Your paragraph would then read:

His goal in life is to be an excellent potter. He works all day forming graceful vases, bowls, and pitchers out of clay. He spends the rest of his time glazing and baking these pots so that they will be beautiful and durable. His teachers say that if he continues working at this rate, he will realize his goal very soon.

471

Now write a paragraph using the following details:

running speed, throwing ability, hitting consistency, hitting with power, thinking ability, fielding ability, coordination, positive attitude, confidence, team spirit, physical condition, clean living.

____

____

____

____

____

____

472

The old man began to tell us the story of his life. When he was fifteen, he ran away to sea. He traveled to South America, China, and Australia. When he was too old to work, he came to this country to live with relatives. Now he talks all the time about the "good old days" when he was young.

Did each sentence in the paragraph tell something about the *man's story* of his *life*?

Answer ____________

(yes) (no

yes

473

We have seen the way that paragraphs are organized around their *subject:* by topic sentence, development, and conclusion.

The paragraph you just read was also organized according to *time.* The old man's story told about four events: his running away to sea, his travels, his retirement to live with relatives, and his talking about the "good old days."

Was the order in which the four events were given in the paragraph the same as or different from the order in which these events occurred in the man's life?

Answer ________________

(same) (different)

same

474

One sentence is out of order in the following paragraph. *Write* the sentence which is out of order.

> His party was a mess. After they all finally left, it took him three hours to clean up. Half of the people he had invited came an hour early. They spilled drinks on his furniture and had a pretzel-eating contest on his bed. Then, someone accidentally set his curtains on fire.

____

____

After they all finally left, it took him three hours to clean up.

475

The sentences below could be put together to form a paragraph. *Number each sentence* according to its time order (1, 2, 3, etc.).

______ *a.* Then we turned left.

______ *b.* To get to the museum, we started off by taking the subway to 79th Street.

______ *c.* Suddenly, right in front of us was the beautiful building we were looking for!

______ *d.* When we got off the subway, we walked four blocks up Lexington Avenue.

______ *e.* After turning left, we walked what seemed to be an endless distance.

a. 3 *c.* 5 *e.* 4
b. 1 *d.* 2

476

Now put the five sentences in the previous frame together to correct time order to form a paragraph.

Then we turned left.
To get to the museum, we started off by taking the subway to 79th Street.
Suddenly, right in front of us was the beautiful building we were looking for!
When we got off the subway, we walked four blocks up Lexington Avenue.
After turning left, we walked what seemed to be an endless distance.

____

____

____

____

____

____

____

____

____

To get to the museum, we started off by taking the subway to 79th Street. When we got off the subway, we walked four blocks up Lexington Avenue. Then we turned left. After turning left, we walked what seemed to be an endless distance. Suddenly, right in front of us was the beautiful building we were looking for!

477

Write a paragraph, using the sentences below in *correct time order.*

I even thought about changing rooms.
At first I didn't like my roommate much.
Now we're close friends.
Then I realized that the only reason I disliked her was that she was different from the people I grew up with.

____

____

____

____

____

At first I didn't like my roommate much. I even thought about changing rooms. Then I realized that the only reason I disliked her was that she was different from the people I grew up with. Now we're close friends.

478

The following paragraph contains several sentences in incorrect time order. Rewrite the paragraph so that it is correct.

When I first met my English professor, I was impressed by his friendliness. At the end of the course, he even invited our class to his house for dinner. Right away he asked me to talk with him about my reading problems. Throughout the rest of the course, he was as helpful to everyone as he had been to me.

____

____

____

____

____

____

____

When I first met my English professor, I was impressed by his friendliness. Right away he asked me to talk with him about my reading problems. Throughout the rest of the course, he was as helpful to everyone as he had been to me. At the end of the course, he even invited the whole class to his house for dinner.

479

When your paragraph is about a *series of events,* they should be written (*Check the correct answer*):

______ *a.* in any order
______ *b.* in the time order in which they happened

Answer __________
(*a*) or (*b*)

b

We have seen that paragraphs are organized in two ways.

1. Paragraphs usually have a *topic sentence, development sentences,* and a *conclusion.*
2. If a paragraph describes a series of events, it should describe the events in correct *time order.*

Now we will look at a different aspect of paragraphs: the structure of their individual *sentences.*

480

Read the following paragraph:

> The old man began to tell us the story of his life. He was fifteen. He ran away to sea. He traveled to South America, China, and Australia. Then he was too old to work. He came to this country to live with relatives. Now he thinks all the time about the "good old days." He was young then.

1. Is this paragraph organized into *topic sentence*, *development*, and *conclusion*?

Answer ___________
(yes) (no)

2. Does the paragraph express *time order* correctly?

Answer ___________
(yes) (no)

1. yes
2. yes

481

Even though the paragraph in the previous frame develops its topic clearly, it is *not* a good paragraph. Let's see why.

Compare these two paragraphs.

a. The old man began to tell us the story of his life. He was fifteen. He ran away to sea. He traveled to South America, China, and Australia. Then he was too old to work. He came to this country to live with relatives. Now he thinks all the time about the "good old days." He was young then.

b. The old man began to tell us the story of his life. When he was fifteen, he ran away to sea. He traveled to South America, China, and Australia. When he was too old to work, he came to this country to live with relatives. Now he thinks all the time about the "good old days" when he was young.

As you may recall, there are three basic types of sentence structure: simple, compound, and complex. *One* of these paragraphs uses the *same type of sentence* all the way through. Which paragraph is it?

Answer ___________
(*a*) or (*b*)

a

482

Paragraph *a* in the previous frame used the same type of sentence all the way through. If you listed each sentence type in paragraph *a*, your list would look like this:

1. simple 5. simple
2. simple 6. simple
3. simple 7. simple
4. simple 8. simple

Look back to paragraph *b* in the previous frame. If you *listed* the types of sentences used in paragraph *b*, what would your list be?

1. ________________
2. ________________
3. ________________
4. ________________
5. ________________

1. simple
2. complex
3. simple
4. complex
5. complex

483

Paragraph *b* is a better paragraph than paragraph *a* because its sentences show the relationships between ideas more clearly, and because the sentence types make it more interesting.

Read the following paragraph:

> The old man began to tell us the story of his life, and he started with the age of fifteen. He ran away to sea at that age, and he traveled to South America, China, and Australia. He became too old to work, and he came to this country to live with relatives. Now he thinks all the time about the "good old days," and he was young then.

List the type of each sentence in this paragraph (simple, compound, or complex).

1. ________________
2. ________________
3. ________________
4. ________________

1. compound
2. compound
3. compound
4. compound

484

The sentences in the paragraph in the previous frame were all of the same type.

Was the paragraph in the previous frame a good one?

Answer ___________
(yes) (no)

no

485

Why was the paragraph you just read not a good one? (*Check the correct answer.*)

______ *a.* It didn't develop its topic.
______ *b.* Its sentences were all of the same type.
______ *c.* It described events in the wrong time order.

b

To find out for yourself how uninteresting a long string of sentences can be if they are all the same type, use your ears. *Read aloud* a group of simple or compound sentences to hear how they sound. Then you will be able to *hear* why sentence variety is necessary in a good paragraph.

486

Read the following paragraph *aloud.* Then answer the question below.

1. I will never drive a car again. 2. I had an accident today. 3. I was driving up Fourth Avenue. 4. I saw a bright yellow car. 5. It was driven by a little old lady. 6. She obviously didn't see the stop sign. 7. I couldn't stop in time. 8. She ran right into me. 9. Then she called me a "young hoodlum."

In your own words, *why* is this not a good paragraph?

____

____

(Your own words)

All the sentences are of the same type.

487

In the next few frames, we will look at each sentence in the previous paragraph to see how it could be improved. We'll start with sentence 1. "I will never drive a car again."

You probably noticed that all the sentences in the paragraph were *simple sentences.* Sentence 1 is the topic sentence, and the rest of the paragraph goes on to develop it. Its purpose is to give the reader an idea of what the paragraph will be about.

Should the structure of sentence 1 be changed?

Answer ____________
(yes) (no)

no

488

Since sentence 1 is the topic sentence, it is probably a good idea to leave it as a simple sentence. Now let's look at sentences 2 and 3.

I had an accident today. I was driving up Fourth Avenue.

We can change the *type* of sentences 2 and 3 by combining them to make one *complex* sentence. Make *one sentence* out of sentences 2 and 3.

____

____

I had an accident today when I was driving up Fourth Avenue. *or* When I was driving up Fourth Avenue today, I had an accident.

489

Combine sentences 4 and 5 the same way, this time using "which" as a connecting word.

I saw a bright yellow car. It was driven by a little old lady.

____

____

I saw a bright yellow car which was driven by a little old lady.

490

The last two sentences you wrote (combining 2 and 3, and 4 and 5) were both ______________________ sentences.

(simple) (compound) (complex)

complex

491

You have written two *complex* sentences in a row. The next sentence should probably be a different type.

Thus, the next sentence in the paragraph should be either ____________ or ____________ .

(*Either order*)

compound
simple

492

To make your next sentence *simple,* you could just leave sentence 6 as it is:

(6) She obviously didn't see the stop sign.

Instead, let's make it compound. Combine sentence 6 with sentence 7, using the connecting word "and."

(7) I couldn't stop in time.

____

____

She obviously didn't see the stop sign, and I couldn't stop in time.

493

So far, the sentences you have rewritten are: *simple, complex, complex, compound.*

Look now at the last two sentences, 8 and 9:

She ran right into me. Then she called me a "young hoodlum."

These two sentences are obviously supposed to be the climax of the story told in the paragraph. Considering this, and considering the sentence types you have already used, what *type* of sentence or sentences should you end with? (*Check your choice:*)

______ *a.* compound
______ *b.* complex
______ *c.* simple-simple

We think *c*, simple-simple, is the best answer here. This would mean leaving sentences 8 and 9 as they are.

494

We have now developed a series of sentence types: simple, complex, complex, compound, compound, simple, simple.

There could have been a different series of sentence types for this paragraph, of course. Our purpose was to point out that the paragraph could be greatly improved by using sentences that were not all of the same type.

495

Sometimes even *two* sentences of the *same* type sound clumsy, if one follows the other directly.

Read the following three sentences.

1. The house was beautiful. 2. A long sidewalk led up to the door, and rows of flowers stood on each side of the steps. 3. The front of the house was red brick, and the woodwork was painted white.

Which of these three sentences are the same *type*? (*Check the correct answer.*)

______ *a.* 1 and 2
______ *b.* 1 and 3
______ *c.* 2 and 3

c

496

Sentences 2 and 3 are both *compound* sentences.

Here are two ways of changing sentences 2 and 3. Read through each section.

a. The house was beautiful. A long sidewalk led up to the door. Rows of flowers stood on each side of the steps. The front of the house was red brick. The woodwork was painted white.

b. The house was beautiful. A long sidewalk led up to the door, and rows of flowers stood on each side of the steps. The front of the house was red brick with white woodwork.

1. List the *sentence types* in paragraph *a*.

   ______, ______, ______, ______, ______

2. List the *sentence types* in paragraph *b*.

   ______, ______, ______

1. simple, simple, simple, simple, simple
2. simple, compound, simple

497

Which of the paragraphs in the previous frame is the better paragraph?

Answer ______
(*a*) or (*b*)

b

498

Explain, in your own words, why paragraph *b* is the better paragraph.

______

______

(*Your own words*)

Paragraph *b* used different sentence types.

499

Read the following sentences. Suppose that they are the first two sentences in a paragraph.

> Thursday was a sunny day. My brother borrowed a car, and we went to the beach.

Which of the following sentences should probably come next?

a. The water was warm, and we went swimming.
b. Since the water was warm, we went swimming.

Answer __________
(*a*) or (*b*)

If your chose *a*, go to frame 500. If you chose *b*, go to frame 509.

500

Your answer to frame 499 was *a*. Let's see how the three sentences look together.

> Thursday was a sunny day. My brother borrowed a car, and we went to the beach. The water was warm, and we went swimming.

What *type* is each of the three sentences used here?

__________, __________, __________

simple, compound, compound

501

Two compound sentences right next to each other—as in the previous frame—usually are clumsy. If you can, you should try to change one of them to a different type of sentence.

Let's see what would have happened if you had chosen sentence *b*.

Go to the next frame.

no answer required

502

Your three sentences now are all of different *types*.

> Thursday was a sunny day. My brother borrowed a car, and we went to the beach. Since the water was warm, we went swimming.

What *type* is each of the sentences used here?

_____________________, _____________________, _____________________

simple, compound, complex

503

We are not saying that two sentences of the same type should never come next to each other in a paragraph. In the example you just worked on, it was our opinion that two *compound* sentences together sounded clumsy.

The important thing to remember about the sentences in your paragraphs is: (*Check the correct answer.*)

______ *a.* All the sentences should be simple.
______ *b.* All the sentences should be complex.
______ *c.* Never put two compound sentences together.
______ *d.* The sentences should not all be of the same type.

d

504

Change the following sentences so that they would make a good beginning for a paragraph.

> Living in the North is hard in winter. The sun doesn't come up until almost nine. It's dark again by three.

____

____

____

Living in the North is hard in the winter. The sun doesn't come up until almost nine, *and* it's dark again by three.

505

You have learned three points so far about the development sentences in a paragraph. First, they should all relate to the *topic sentence.* Second, if the paragraph traces a series of events, the events should be in correct *time order.*

In your own words, what is the third point?

____

____

(*Your own words*)

The sentences should not all be of the same *type.*

506

The following paragraph has all three types of mistakes. First read it through. Then, cross out the sentence that doesn't belong.

> Bob owes me twenty dollars. He borrowed it a month ago. He hasn't paid me back yet. He crossed the street to avoid me. Today I saw him walking past the bank. When I finally caught up with him, he said that he could pay me on Friday. I'm a very fast walker. If he doesn't pay me then, I'll have to start charging interest.

Bob owes me twenty dollars. He borrowed it a month ago. He hasn't paid me back yet. He crossed the street to avoid me. Today I saw him walking past the bank. When I finally caught up with him, he said that he could pay me on Friday. ~~I'm a very fast walker.~~ If he doesn't pay me then, I'll have to start charging interest.

507

Now rewrite the following paragraph. Correct the *time order* of the sentences.

> Bob owes me twenty dollars. He borrowed it a month ago. He hasn't paid me back yet. He crossed the street to avoid me. Today I saw him walking past the bank. When I finally caught up with him, he said that he could pay me on Friday. If he doesn't pay me then, I'll have to start charging interest.

____

____

____

____

Bob owes me twenty dollars. He borrowed it a month ago. He hasn't paid me back yet. Today I saw him walking past the bank. He crossed the street to avoid me. When I finally caught up with him, he said that he could pay me on Friday. If he doesn't pay me then, I'll have to start charging interest.

508

Now rewrite the following paragraph. Connect sentences 2 and 3 to form a new type of sentence.

> Bob owes me twenty dollars. He borrowed it a month ago. He hasn't paid me back yet. Today I saw him walking past the bank. He crossed the street to avoid me. When I finally caught up with him, he said that he could pay me on Friday. If he doesn't pay me then, I'll have to start charging interest.

Bob owes me twenty dollars. He borrowed it a month ago, and he hasn't paid me back yet. Today I saw him walking past the bank. He crossed the street to avoid me. When I finally caught up with him, he said that he could pay me on Friday. If he doesn't pay me then, I'll have to start charging interest.

The individual sentences in a paragraph all relate to each other as well as to the topic sentence. The ideal paragraph, if there is such a thing, contains sentences that follow each other logically to a conclusion. There are several ways to *emphasize* the relationship of each sentence to the next sentence. The next several frames will provide you with techniques for emphasizing sentence relationships.

509

Read these two sentences:

I was an innocent child. My parents sheltered me.

The ideas in the two sentences are *related* to each other. As they are written, though, it is up to the reader to guess exactly how they are related.

Suppose you wanted to *connect* these two sentences, using a connecting word showing that being sheltered was the cause of the child's innocence. Which of the following connecting words do you think would be *best*?

______ *a.* and
______ *b.* because
______ *c.* although
______ *d.* but

b

510

Now connect the two sentences, using the connecting word "because."

I was an innocent child. My parents sheltered me.

____

____

I was an innocent child because my parents sheltered me.

511

Connect the following two sentences, using the connecting word "although."

I kept on visiting her parents. I didn't like to.

____

____

I kept on visiting her parents although I didn't like to.

512

If there are sentences in your paragraphs whose relationship to each other *could* be shown more clearly, try combining them with the right connecting word.

Two sentences in the following paragraph could be improved by connecting them with a connecting word. Decide which two sentences can be combined and rewrite the paragraph.

At the bottom of the ocean, darkness is absolute. Beyond 2,000 feet there is no light at all. The sun's rays cannot go deeper than 2,000 feet. Probably the only men who can imagine this blackness are the few men who have actually seen it.

At the bottom of the ocean, darkness is absolute. Beyond 2,000 feet there is no light at all, *because* the sun's rays cannot go deeper than 2,000 feet. Probably the only men who can imagine this blackness are the few men who have actually seen it.

513

The word "because" is a connecting word used to combine two sentences. You can also use words that show *transition*—to carry over a thought from one sentence to another. In using a transition word to emphasize a relationship between two sentences, the sentences need not be combined—but can remain separate sentences.

Read the sentences below. *Write* the word that shows *transition* from the first sentence to the second.

He forgot there was a test today. Consequently, he failed.

consequently

514

Without the transition word, the sentences in the previous frame would have been:

He forgot there was a test today. He failed.

Notice that you also *could* have made the relationship clearer by using a connecting word to combine the two sentences.

He failed because he forgot there was a test today.

Rewrite the following sentences:

He ate a whole pie. He got sick.

1. by combining them (use the connecting word "because")

____

____

2. by using a *transition* word (use "consequently").

____

____

1. He got sick *because* he ate a whole pie.
2. He ate a whole pie. Consequently, he got sick.

515

Rewrite the following sets of sentences using the *transition* word "consequently" to show the relationships between them.

1. Her husband died. She is a widow.

____

____

2. We took the wrong exit. We got lost.

____

____

3. Their father lost his job. They had to move.

____

____

1. Her husband died. Consequently, she is a widow.
2. We took the wrong exit. Consequently, we got lost.
3. Their father lost his job. Consequently, they had to move.

516

"Consequently" is a transition word that shows a *cause-and-effect* relationship. (One sentence is a consequence of another one.) There are many other useful transition words.

Write the transition word used in the following sentences.

He was very handsome. Also, he was very intelligent.

____

also

517

Does "also" in the previous frame show a *cause-and-effect* relationship?

Answer ____________
(yes) (no)

no

518

Different transition words show different relationships between sentences.

In frame 516, the transition word was "also." This showed that you wanted to give *more* information about your subject than just the fact that he was handsome.

Rewrite the sets of sentences below, using "also" as a transition word.

1. The trip is long. It is dangerous.

____

____

2. Our car has a flat tire. The radiator leaks.

____

____

1. The trip is long. Also, it is dangerous.
2. Our car has a flat tire. Also, the radiator leaks.

519

Below are two examples of sentences that need transition words. Decide whether the relationship between the sentences in each example is a "consequently" relationship or an "also" relationship and *rewrite* the sentences correctly.

1. He is only 5 feet tall. He cannot be a policeman.

____

____

2. He is only 5 feet tall. He is bald.

____

____

1. He is only 5 feet tall. Consequently, he cannot be a policeman.
2. He is only 5 feet tall. Also, he is bald.

520

Use both "also" and "consequently" to show the relationships among the following three sentences. *Rewrite* the three sentences.

He is only 5 feet tall. He is bald. I don't want to go out with him.

____

____

____

He is only 5 feet tall. Also, he is bald. Consequently, I don't want to go out with him.

521

There are also *phrases* that show transition. Write the *phrase* that shows transition in the sentence below.

She told us many exciting stories. For example, she told us about the Loch Ness monster.

____

for example

522

"For example" is a transition phrase to tell the reader that you are going to give him an *example* or an *illustration.*

Rewrite the following sets of sentences, using "for example" as a transition phrase.

1. She is very well educated. She has two graduate degrees.

____

____

2. This is an expensive hotel. The smallest room is forty dollars a day.

____

____

1. She is very well educated. For example, she has two graduate degrees.
2. That is an expensive hotel. For example, the smallest room is forty dollars a day.

523

There are many useful transition words and phrases. Some of them show similar relationships.

Read the following sets of sentences.

a. He dieted for a month. Consequently, he lost weight.
b. He dieted for a month. As a result, he lost weight.

Is the relationship between the sentences in *a* different from the relationship between the sentences in *b*?

Answer ____________
(yes) (no)

no

524

Rewrite the following two sentences, this time using "also" as a transition word.

He studied all night. Consequently, he studied all night the night before last.

He studied all last night. Also, he studied all night the night before last.

525

Here is an *extreme example* of what can happen when transition words are used incorrectly.

He is very handsome. Consequently, he is very intelligent.

These sentences imply that he is intelligent *because* he is handsome. Probably what the writer meant was that he was intelligent *as well as* handsome. If so, "also" would have been a better transition word to use.

There is one kind of transition word which is *especially* confusing if used incorrectly.

Write the transition word used in these two sentences.

He is usually very dependable. However, he didn't show up today.

____

however

526

The transition word "however" indicates that you are going to make a statement that in some way *contradicts*—or is an *exception* to—your first statement. In the previous frame, you said that he is usually dependable, *but* he *didn't* show up today.

Read the following sets of sentences.

a. He is my best friend. Sometimes he really makes me furious.
b. He is my best friend. We do everything together.

Which of the above sets of sentences could use the transition word "*however*"?

Answer ____________
(*a*) or (*b*)

a

527

Rewrite these two sentences, using the transition word "however."

He is my best friend. Sometimes he really makes me furious.

He is my best friend. However, sometimes he really makes me furious.

528

When you want to make a statement that *contradicts* in some way—or is an exception to—a statement you made earlier, be sure to warn your readers by using transition words like "however" or "nevertheless." If you don't, you are likely to be misunderstood.

Rewrite the following sentences so that their relationship is clear. Use a *transition word.*

She is often late. I won't fire her.

She is often late. However, (*or* nevertheless,) I won't fire her.

529

Rewrite the following sets of sentences, using the transition word "however."

1. We wanted to go swimming. It rained.

---

2. I said I'd call him. I was too busy.

---

3. George is very bright. He never studies.

---

1. We wanted to go swimming. However, it rained.
2. I said I'd call him. However, I was too busy.
3. George is very bright. However, he never studies.

530

In the past several frames, you learned two ways of showing relationships between sentences: using connecting words to combine two sentences and using transition words to introduce the second of the two sentences. Even though the functions of connecting words and transition words are similar, you must be careful not to confuse the two.

Which of the following is *correct*?

a. We called him. However, he wasn't home.
b. We called him, however, he wasn't home.

Answer ____________
(*a*) or (*b*)

a

531

Which of the following is *correct*?

a. She called me because she was going to be late.
b. She called me. Because, she was going to be late.

Answer ____________
(*a*) or (*b*)

a

532

In the previous frame, sentence *b* used "because" as if it were a *transition* word. However, it is a *connecting* word and should have joined the sentences as in *a*.

Rewrite the following sentences so that they are *correct*.

1. We called him, however, he wasn't home.

____

____

2. She called me. Because, she was going to be late.

1. We called him. However, he wasn't home.
2. She called me because she was going to be late.

533

Make correct sentences out of the following elements.

1. We invited him also we invited his brother

2. Steve is out of town nevertheless we should do what he asked

3. Our basement is flooded although it hasn't rained

4. We are tired because we studied all night

5. She is very busy however she will see you

1. We invited him. Also, we invited his brother.
2. Steve is out of town. Nevertheless, we should do what he asked.
3. Our basement is flooded although it hasn't rained.
4. We are tired because we studied all night.
5. She is very busy. However, she will see you.

534

The following paragraph contains *incorrectly used* connecting or transition words. There are also places where a connecting or transition word is *needed* to show relationships between sentences. Correct the incorrect sentences, and supply words where they are needed.

> When we arrived, the weather was bitter cold. The cabin had a gas heater, however, there was no gas. We were angry at each other. We had forgotten the blankets. Finally, we discovered an old wood stove and some firewood. After we got a fire started, the cabin was as warm as summer. We decided not to visit there again until spring.

____

____

____

____

____

____

____

____

____

____

When we arrived, the weather was bitter cold. The cabin had a gas heater. *However,* there was no gas. We were angry at each other *because* we had forgotten the blankets. Finally, we discovered an old wood stove and some firewood. After we got a fire started, the cabin was as warm as summer. However, (*or* Nevertheless,) we decided not to visit there again until spring.

535

You have looked at several aspects of the sentences that develop the idea of a paragraph. You know that the development sentences should be in correct time order, relate to the subject of the paragraph, and be of varied types. You also have learned how to use transition words and connecting words to emphasize the relationships between facts.

In the next three frames, you will practice using some of these guides to writing effective development sentences.

536

In this frame, we will supply you with a topic sentence, a conclusion, and some facts. Use the facts in the table below to lead the topic sentence to the conclusion. Write your development sentences in the lines provided.

A study has been made to determine whether the level of water pollution in Beekman County has increased or decreased during the last fifteen years.

____

____

____

____

This indicates that water pollution has increased enormously.

Beekman County	*1955*	*1970*
Number of streams	30	30
Number of swimming streams	25	0
Number of fishing streams	30	0

The study showed that in 1955, people could fish in all thirty streams and swim in most of them. Today, you can't fish or swim in any of them.

537

In this frame, we will give you a *topic sentence* and a *series of events.* Finish the paragraph on the lines provided, using transition words to show the sequence of events.

Events:
1. The committee leaders gave reports.
2. The reports were discussed.
3. People made suggestions about floats.
4. The meeting was adjourned at nine o'clock.

Our last meeting before the parade was interesting. ____________________

____

____

____

____

____

Your paragraph should contain sentences describing the events *in this order.*

Our last meeting before the parade was interesting. First, the committee leaders gave reports. Then, the reports were discussed, and people made suggestions about floats to the committees. The meeting was adjourned at nine o'clock.

538

In this frame, we will give you a topic sentence, some facts, and a conclusion. Finish the paragraph. (*Use the following diagram.*)

George read a special book which he hoped would teach him to spell better.

____

____

____

____

____

____

____

____

____

Reading the book obviously helped his spelling.

	Before reading book	*After reading book*
Number of words spelled wrong on test	33	13

George read a special book which he hoped would teach him to spell better. Before he read the book, he had spelled thirty-three words wrong on a test. After he read the book, he spelled thirteen words wrong on the same test. Reading the book obviously helped his spelling.

539

In this frame, we will give you a topic sentence, some facts, and a conclusion. Finish the paragraph. (*Use the following diagram.*)

At one end of our block is a very dangerous intersection.

Having the stop sign there decreased the number of accidents immediately.

	Year before stop sign was put up	*Year after stop sign was put up*
Number of accidents per year	90	23

Your answer should be similar to this:

At one end of our block is a very dangerous intersection. Before a stop sign was put up, there were ninety accidents there in a year. After a stop sign was put up, there were only twenty-three accidents in a year. Having the stop sign there decreased the number of accidents immediately.

540

In this frame, we will give you a topic sentence and some facts. Finish the paragraph.

My sister dieted for three months.

____

____

__________________. The diet definitely helped her lose weight.

	September	December
My sister's weight	145 lb	120 lb

Your paragraph should be similar to this one:

My sister dieted for three months. When she started in September, she weighed 145 pounds. By December, she was down to 120 pounds. The diet definitely helped her lose weight.

The previous frames gave you some basic guidelines for organizing and constructing development sentences in paragraph writing. Besides topic sentences and development sentences, many paragraphs require a sentence that sums up the facts in your paragraph. We will refer to such sentences as *conclusions* or *concluding sentences.*

When you complete the following frames, you will be able to write appropriate concluding sentences for your paragraphs.

541

Not all paragraphs need concluding sentences. There are no strict rules to tell you which paragraphs need concluding sentences and which ones don't. In the next several frames, we offer you some general guides to help you decide.

Go to the next frame.

no answer required

542

A paragraph is likely to need a concluding sentence if the paragraph exists by itself—that is, it is *not* a part of a larger story or paper. In other words, if you want to develop an idea in *one* paragraph, you will probably need to write a conclusion at the end of the paragraph.

For example, in one of the preceding exercises, you wrote a paragraph about a study of water pollution in a particular country. You showed that fifteen years ago only one of the nearby streams was polluted, and that today they all are. Was a conclusion needed?

Answer ____________
(yes) (no)

yes

(You needed to conclude that the pollution problem had increased enormously.)

543

Often, key words in the topic sentence can be picked up and used for the conclusion. The conclusion may answer *questions* suggested by the topic sentence.

Read the paragraph below.

> A study has been made of how the level of water pollution in Beekman County has changed during the last fifteen years. The study showed that in 1955, it was still possible to swim and fish in most of the streams within 10 miles of here. Today, swimming is out of the question, and there are no more fish in any of these streams. This indicates that water pollution has increased enormously.

What are the *key words* in:

1. the topic sentence?

 ____

2. the concluding sentence?

 ____

Your answer should include at least these words:

1. study, water pollution, changed
2. water pollution, increased

544

In the previous paragraph, the concluding sentence answered the question suggested by the topic sentence: "Has water pollution in the county increased or decreased?"

Read the following topic sentence:

> Our old neighborhood is different from the way it used to be.

1. What are the key words in the topic sentence?

____

2. What *question* does the topic sentence suggest? (*In your own words*)

____

1. "neighborhood," "different"
2. (*Your own words*) *How* is the neighborhood different?

545

Now read the following paragraph, keeping in mind the question "How is the neighborhood different?"

> Our old neighborhood is different from the way it used to be. When I last visited there, about half the homes had been torn down to make way for a superhighway. The remaining buildings were plastered with billboards and surrounded by traffic signs and litter.

What do you think might be possible *key words* for a concluding sentence to this paragraph?

____

Your words should have been something like "neighborhood," "dirty," "noisy," "full of cars," and so on.

546

Using the *key words* in answer 545, write a possible concluding sentence for the paragraph in the previous frame.

____

____

Your sentence should have been similar to:

Now, the whole neighborhood has become dirty, noisy, and full of cars.

547

If your paragraph is well developed, it should lead directly to a conclusion. However, some paragraphs—especially those that are part of a series of paragraphs—do not follow our basic pattern of topic-development-conclusion. For example, some paragraphs may not start with a topic sentence. In such case, the *purpose* of the paragraph should be stated—either at the beginning or the end—to serve as *both* a topic sentence and a conclusion.

Read the following paragraph.

> First, I would like to meet people from outside my home town. Second, I would like to learn about things I can't learn about on a job. Third, I would like to have an interesting job someday rather than a dull job that will just support me.

Do you think this paragraph states its purpose?

Answer ____________
(yes) (no)

no

548

The paragraph in the previous frame needs a sentence either at the beginning or at the end to state its purpose. Suppose the purpose of the paragraph was to answer the question. Why do you want to go to college?

Which of the following sentences do you think would make a good *concluding* sentence for the paragraph in the previous frame? (*Check the correct answer.*)

______ *a.* I don't have enough money for college.
______ *b.* College never interested me much.
______ *c.* These are the three main reasons why I want to go to college.
______ *d.* There are three main reasons why I want to go to college.

c (Sentence *d* would make a good *opening* topic sentence.)

549

What do you think is the *purpose* of this paragraph? (*Check the correct answer.*)

> Wherever they ruled, the Romans made Latin a common language. They brought Roman law and Roman citizenship. They took native men into the Roman army. Key cities and highways were built to consolidate their power.

______ *a.* to show how people lived in ancient Rome
______ *b.* to show how the Romans organized their empire
______ *c.* to show how Rome fell from power

b

550

Read the paragraph again, keeping in mind its purpose of showing how well the Romans organized their empire. Then, *write* a sentence at the end that serves as *both* a topic sentence and a conclusion.

> Wherever they ruled, the Romans made Latin a common language. They brought Roman law and Roman citizenship. They took native men into the Roman army. Key cities and highways were built to consolidate their power.

____

____

Your concluding sentence should be similar to:

These methods helped the Romans organize their empire well. *or,* The Romans organized their empire well. *or* (simply) That was how the Romans organized their empire.

551

We said earlier that *transition words* could be used to show relationships between sentences. There are also transition words to introduce concluding sentences.

In the blank below, write the words that tell you this is a concluding sentence.

> In conclusion, it seems definitely advisable for you to take the job.

____

In conclusion

552

The phrase "In conclusion" shows the relationship between a concluding sentence and the rest of the paragraph. It tells the reader that you are going to *sum up* what you have just said.

In the blank below, write the phrase that tells you that the following sentence is a concluding sentence.

> In short, it was a very disturbing play.

____

In short

553

Other transition phrases that indicate a *conclusion* are "to sum up" and "to conclude." Phrases like these do not have to introduce *every* concluding sentence. They are most helpful when your paragraph has listed several facts and you want to tie them all together in the conclusion.

Go to the next frame.

no answer required

554

Read the following paragraph. Then, *write* a concluding sentence for it, using a *transition phrase.*

> During the Middle Ages, classes at the University of Paris began at 5 a.m. All morning students attended their regular class lectures, and all afternoon they attended special lectures. After twelve hours of classes, the sudents had sports events. Then came homework—copying, recopying, and memorizing notes.

____

____

Sample answer:

In short (In conclusion, To sum up, etc.), the school day at the University of Paris was a long and hard one.

Most of the paragraphs you write will *not* be single paragraphs. They will be part of a series of paragraphs which combine to form a story, a paper, a letter, and so on. When you write a series of paragraphs, you will need to show the *relationship* between them.

We will look now at a different use of concluding sentences: to show relationships in a series of paragraphs.

555

Read the following paragraph:

> Statistics since 1960 show that the amount of poverty in the county is increasing. In 1960, 11 percent of the population fell below the poverty line. In 1966, the figure was 14 percent. Still, there are signs now that the trend toward poverty may be slowing down.

What are the *key words* in the *concluding* sentence?

You should have at least: "trend" and "slowing down."

556

Key words in the concluding sentence in the previous paragraph were "trend" and "slowing down." These key words contradict the statistics in the first part of the paragraph. This leads you to think that the purpose of the concluding sentence *in the previous frame* is: (*Check the correct answer.*)

______ *a.* to sum up
______ *b.* to point toward a new paragraph

b

557

Read the concluding sentence again:

> Still, there are signs now that the trend toward poverty may be slowing down.

What would you expect the *next* paragraph to be about? (*Check the correct answer.*)

______ *a.* signs that poverty is spreading faster and faster
______ *b.* signs that poverty is increasing at a slower rate
______ *c.* signs that poverty has been eliminated

b

558

What part of the paragraph in frame 555 gave you the clue to what the following paragraph might be about? (*Check the correct answer.*)

______ *a.* topic sentence
______ *b.* connecting words
______ *c.* concluding sentence

c

559

In a *series* of paragraphs, one purpose of a concluding sentence in one of the paragraphs would be (*In your own words*):

____

____

(*Your own words*)

to indicate what the next paragraph is about.

560

Read the paragraph again:

> Statistics since 1960 show that the amount of poverty in the county is increasing. In 1960, 11 percent of the population fell below the poverty line. In 1966, the figure was 14 percent. Still, there are signs now that the trend toward poverty may be slowing down.

Which of the following paragraphs could *logically* follow this paragraph?

a. In fact, statistics since 1966 indicate that poverty is increasing faster than ever. Unemployment has risen, and no new industries have plans to move into the area. These facts indicate that the poverty problem will grow worse instead of better.

b. A few signs of improvement are rising employment, rising educational levels, and the increasing number of agencies providing emergency job and educational help. These tendencies lead to the hope that poverty can be held down.

Answer ____________
(*a*) or (*b*)

b

The concluding sentence in the first paragraph indicated that the second paragraph would be about signs that might *contradict* the past trend of rising poverty. Paragraph *b* did list these signs.

561

Read the following two paragraphs. A concluding sentence is missing in the first paragraph. *Write* a concluding sentence that will provide a transition to the second paragraph.

> There are very few inexpensive places to visit on a weekend. Most of the mountain or ocean resort areas create as much financial strain as they do physical relaxation. ______________________________________
>
> ____

One of these exceptions is a weekend visit to the natural caverns in our region. Touring the caves is always interesting, and the surrounding areas usually have space for picnics. I always enjoy these visits and come home with some money left, too.

Your sentence should be similar to one of these:

However, there are a few exceptions to this rule.
However, there are some places that are not expensive.

562

Read the following two paragraphs. Write a concluding sentence for the first paragraph which will provide a transition to the second paragraph.

As the votes were counted, our anxiety grew. Had Jones, our candidate, won? From time to time someone would emerge from the office to tell us how the count was going. It seemed to be lasting forever. ____________

____

____

After so many hours of waiting, the relief was overwhelming. People laughed, clapped, and kissed each other. After about an hour of celebration we all went home—tired but happy.

Your answer should be similar to this:

Finally the result was announced: Jones had won.

563

The following piece of writing has not been broken up into paragraphs, but it should be. Read it through and look for places where the development of one statement ends and another begins. At these places (where different ideas or topics are introduced) new paragraphs should begin. Make a slash mark (/) at these places. Check your work with your instructor.

For two months I had been exchanging glances with a blonde who looked good enough to put those centerfold types to shame. I didn't really know what to say to her; women that look that good cause my tongue to do funny things. Suddenly I forget what meager vocabulary I ever knew and emit monosyllabic grunts that I hope will pass for words. Anyhow, today changed all that. . . .forever, I hope! I was standing in line trying to register for my second semester courses when that blonde of my fantasies appeared at my elbow. I looked down at her and before I could go into my usual numb tongue routine, she said, "Hey handsome, who would be good to take for English Composition?" My flattered ego unstuck my tongue and I mumbled that Masters was supposed to be excellent; that he used music and contemporary media as background for writing. She said, "sounds good; you gonna take him?" I beamed in on her pretty well with my eyes, which I hoped told her volumes more than my muffled "yeah." We got into a fine conversation after that, mostly centering around our common interest in music. Tonight she and I are going dancing and I have a feeling that things are going to be fine between us for a long time to come. . . .

In the last several frames, you have seen examples of several ways to connect paragraphs. When you write a paper, you must first organize your paragraphs in logical order so that the connections will make sense.

Section 6 Organizing Essays

564

When you write a paper, you should *organize* the information in it so that people can read and understand it easily. If your information isn't organized clearly, the points you want to make may be lost.

Suppose you are comparing two papers. *Paper A* is organized in this way:

Paragraph 1: Question
Paragraph 2: Evidence
Paragraph 3: Evidence
Paragraph 4: Conclusion

Paper B is organized in this way:

Paragraph 1: Evidence
Paragraph 2: Conclusion
Paragraph 3: Question
Paragraph 4: Evidence

Which paper would be easier to understand?

Answer ________
A or *B*

A

565

A paper that asks a question, gives evidence, and then comes to a conclusion is easy to understand.

Read the following four short paragraphs:

a. For instance, fifteen years ago the creeks in this county were all clean enough to swim in. Now, they have signs to warn people that swimming in them is dangerous.

b. To find out the facts about water pollution, look around at the area in which you live. Examine the condition of the water over a long period of time. Then you can decide whether the pollution level has changed or not.

c. From these two observations, it seems obvious that water pollution has greatly increased in our county. The same might be true of the rest of the nation. If it is, we can only conclude that we will someday be faced with a crisis in our water supply.

d. Also, fifteen years ago there were plenty of fish in the nearby streams. Fishermen say that today there are only a few places in which fish can still survive.

Write the *letter* of each paragraph in the order that you think would make a clear paper.

1. ______
2. ______
3. ______
4. ______

1. *b*
2. *a*
3. *d*
4. *c*

At first, the paragraphs in this frame were in this order: evidence, question, conclusion, evidence. This order was confusing to read. We changed the order of the paragraphs to: question, evidence, evidence, conclusion. This made the point about increased water pollution clear.

566

When you write, try to decide beforehand what you want to say. (You saw that the first step in writing a paragraph was to decide what it was to be *about.*) When you write a letter, a paper, or a story, you should also know what you want to say in order to be able to organize it.

Suppose you are writing a report on a neighborhood meeting you attended. The events at the meeting happened in this order:

1. people introduced themselves
2. the group talked about its reason for meeting
3. the group elected officers
4. the group decided when to meet again
5. the meeting adjourned

How many *paragraphs* will probably be in your report? ________________

five

567

Referring to the material in the previous frame, which of the following ways of organizing your five paragraphs would be best? (*Check the correct answer.*)

______ *a.* by length
______ *b.* by importance
______ *c.* by time order

c

568

A report on a meeting is fairly simple to organize, since you would usually want to describe events in the order in which they happened. However, many papers and stories are harder to organize.

Suppose you are writing a story about something that happened once in a town where you used to live. You want to include the following things:

a. a description of the town
b. a description of the event
c. a description of the people involved in the event
d. the results of the event

Of course, any one of these things could be told in any number of paragraphs. But in what *order* do you think *a, b, c* and *d* should be in your story?

1. ______
2. ______
3. ______
4. ______

1. *a*
2. *c*
3. *b*
4. *d*

569

Once you have *organized* your expository paper, letter, or story, you can use paragraphs to separate one subject or idea from another. Then, people who read what you've written can follow your reasoning easily. Notice that this is also true in a descriptive paragraph situation. Observe where the paragraph breaks are in the following correct story-model.

Love surely changes your perspective on things! There's this beautiful woman I've been dating for about three months now. We've got a great thing going, but I was a little "up tight" about what would happen when spring semester break occurred. She's very romantic and loves to write letters. While we were together there was no threat because my secret was safe . . . I was never good at writing. I panicked whenever I thought of revealing my awkward thinking to my lady love.

Today all that changed! My favorite teacher, an up-to-date English professor by the name of Peek, introduced us to poetry writing. She said that it was possible to express your feelings in an open, nonthreatening form. Spurred on by my desire to write romantically, I made my first effort at poetry writing. Amazingly, I felt comfortable doing it. She taught us a structural poetic form called "haiku" that just seemed to flow from my mind. There are three lines in the poem: five syllables in the first line, seven syllables in the second line, and five syllables in the third line. Here's what my first effort looked like:

Lover, I need you . . .
Your sensuous, kind nature
captures my soul!

I may not be Percy Bysshe Shelley yet, but at least I'm willing to try writing over spring vacation. Who says college doesn't help you?!

570

Read the three paragraphs below. They contain three developed ideas, but the paragraphs begin and end in the wrong places. They do not *separate the ideas clearly.* Rewrite the paragraphs so that the ideas are clearly separated.

There are many ideas about how the world was created. The earliest theories about the creation are usually found in ancient books which have been passed down through the years. These books describe how early people believed the earth was formed. The myths of the Scandinavians come from two books called the *Eddas.*

According to the *Eddas,* the world was created from a bottomless ocean.

An icy fountain arose from the bottomless ocean and caused a mist to fall, which became land. Two other ideas about the earth are found in the Book of Genesis in the Bible. One says that the earth was created out of desert, and the other says that the earth was created from an ocean.

There are many ideas about how the world was created. The earliest theories about the creation are usually found in ancient books which have been passed down through the years. These books describe how early people believed the earth was formed.

The myths of the Scandinavians come from two books called the *Eddas*. According to the *Eddas,* the world was created from a bottomless ocean. An icy fountain arose from the bottomless ocean and caused a mist to fall, which became land.

Two other ideas about the earth are found in the Book of Genesis in the Bible. One says that the earth was created out of desert, and the other says that the earth was created from an ocean.

571

In frame 570, the ideas were not separated clearly into paragraphs. When you changed the paragraphs, it became clear that:

The first paragraph was about ancient books and their theories *in general.*

1. The second paragraph was about

   ____

2. The third paragraph was about

   ____

(*Your own words*)

1. the theories in the *Eddas*
2. the theories in the Bible

572

Write out the *sentences* in frame 570 that introduce the following topics:

1. theories in the *Eddas*

   ____

   ____

2. theories in the Bible

   ____

   ____

1. The myths of the Scandinavians come from two books called the *Eddas.*
2. Two other ideas about the earth are found in the Book of Genesis in the Bible.

573

In their own paragraphs, these two sentences are: (*Check the correct answer.*)

______ *a.* topic sentences
______ *b.* concluding sentences
______ *c.* development sentences

a

574

We saw earlier that the *concluding sentence* of one paragraph could be used to point toward a new paragraph. Now we see that *topic sentences* can be used to make the same kind of connection between paragraphs.

Topic sentences in a series of paragraphs can be used: (*Check all that apply.*)

______ *a.* to make conclusions
______ *b.* to introduce paragraphs about different ideas
______ *c.* to show connections between paragraphs

b, c

575

Read the following paragraphs:

> The growth of office buildings in downtown Manhattan threatens to make the area good for only one thing: working in an office. The new pattern is to build "slabs" of offices reaching into the sky, with none of the tiny restaurants, shops, or other services that make an area interesting.
>
> This building pattern can ruin the benefits illustrated in the theater district. The low buildings offer two gifts to a pedestrian: the ability to see where he is, and a variety of small stores and theaters he can enjoy. The number of new office buildings planned for this area would eliminate both of these advantages.

Read the *topic sentence* of the second paragraph.

1. What *key words* in the topic sentence refer back to an idea in the *first* paragraph?

   ____

2. What *key words* in the topic sentence point ahead to what the *second* paragraph will be about?

   ____

1. (This) building pattern
2. theater district

576

In the last several frames, we have shown the importance of organizing your ideas into paragraphs and showing the relationships between paragraphs.

The following sentences can be reorganized to make three paragraphs. *Organize them* according to their three subjects, and write your three *paragraphs* below (you won't have to rewrite any sentences).

There are several recent city designs that have made improvements in city life. These improvements give pedestrians more room to walk, more variety in what they see, and less trouble with nearby traffic. In 1931, Rockefeller Center was begun. This area uses a wide underground pathway for pedestrians. This pathway is lined with shops and restaurants, and since it is underground, it avoids all the street-level traffic. More recently, several apartment and office towers have been built in London. These towers have a pedestrian pathway which is raised *above* the street. This pathway, like Rockefeller Center, is lined with plazas and shops.

There are several recent city designs that have made improvements in city life. These improvements give pedestrians more room to walk, more variety in what they see, and less trouble with nearby traffic.

In 1931, Rockefeller Center was begun. This area uses a wide underground pathway for pedestrians. This pathway is lined with shops and restaurants, and since it is underground, it avoids all the street-level traffic.

More recently, several apartment and office towers have been built in London. These towers have a pedestrian pathway which is raised *above* the street. This pathway, like Rockefeller Center, is lined with plazas and shops.

577
Organize the sentences below into two paragraphs. Write your new paragraphs in the space provided.

Every large city has a section where shopping is still done in the old way: on the street. In these sections, storekeepers set out their goods on sidewalk tables. Peddlers push through the crowds of shoppers, and on every corner stands a seller of candy or ice cream. In New York City, one of the best known of these market sections is the Lower East Side. This area, between Delancey and Houston Streets, becomes a real bazaar on Sundays, with merchandise of every kind for sale along the sidewalks. It is a piece of the Old World in the center of twentieth-century commerce.

Every large city has a section where shopping is still done in the old way: on the street. In these sections, storekeepers set out their goods on sidewalk tables. Peddlers push through the crowds of shoppers, and on every corner stands a seller of candy or ice cream.

In New York City, one of the best known of these market sections is the Lower East Side. This area, between Delancey and Houston Streets, becomes a real bazaar on Sundays, with merchandise of every kind for sale along the sidewalks. It is a piece of the Old World in the center of twentieth-century commerce.

Section 7 Rewriting and Editing

No matter how careful you are when you write there will always be some mistakes that you miss. For this reason, it is important for you to know how to check over what you write. When you finish this chapter, you will be able to use effective rereading and revising techniques to improve your own writing.

578

You don't want to become too afraid of making mistakes when you write the first version of a paper. If you do, you may not get around to expressing your ideas. However, this shows why *re*writing is so important: it allows you to go back over your work and correct things like paragraph organization, sentence structure, and punctuation separately.

Eventually, correct writing will become easier for you if you: (*Check the correct answer.*)

______ *a.* leave your first pieces of writing as they are
______ *b.* go back and check what you write for mistakes
______ *c.* wait until someone corrects you

b

579

Rewriting may seem like a huge amount of work. If you tried to correct everything at once, it probably would be. The solution is to take one step at a time.

A helpful *first* step is to read through your whole letter, paper, story, and so on for *sense only*—without worrying about grammar. This step would help you see: (*Check the correct answer.*)

______ *a.* if your overall idea is clear
______ *b.* if your commas are used correctly
______ *c.* if your subjects and verbs agree

a

580

If you have reread your paper for sense only and you aren't sure whether or not your point is clear, try this: go through your paper and *underline* the first sentence in each paragraph. Then read *only the underlined sentences* to see if they show connected ideas.

Try this technique on four paragraphs we have read before. *Underline* and *read the first sentence* in each paragraph below.

> To find out the facts about water pollution, look around at the area in which you live. Examine the condition of the water over a long period of time. Then you can decide whether the pollution level has changed or not.
>
> For instance, now there are signs at the creeks to warn people that swimming in them is dangerous. Fifteen years ago they were all clean enough to swim in.
>
> Also, today there are only a few places in which fish can still survive. Fifteen years ago there were plenty of fish in the nearby streams.
>
> From these two observations, it seems obvious that water pollution has greatly increased in our county. The same might be true of the rest of the nation. If it is, we can only *conclude* that we will someday be faced with a crisis in our water supply.

<u>To find out the facts about water pollution, look around at the area in which you live.</u>

<u>For instance, now there are signs at the creeks to warn people that swimming in them is dangerous.</u>

<u>Also, today there are only a few places in which fish can still survive.</u>

<u>From these two observations, it seems obvious that water pollution has greatly increased in our county.</u>

581

Read the four topic sentences together:

> To find out the facts about water pollution, look around at the area in which you live. For instance, now there are signs at the creeks to warn people that swimming in them is dangerous. Also, today there are only a few places in which fish can still survive. From these two observations, it seems obvious that water pollution has greatly increased in our county.

Are these sentences a logical framework for the point made in the conclusion: "we can only *conclude* that we will someday be faced with a crisis in our water supply."

Answer ____________
(yes) (no)

yes

582

Suppose you found that your four topic sentences were in this order:

> To find out the facts about water pollution, look around at the area in which you live.
>
> For instance, now there are signs at the creeks to warn people that swimming in them is dangerous.
>
> From these two observations, it seems obvious that water pollution has greatly increased in our county.
>
> Also, today there are only a few places in which fish can still survive.

You would see that: (*Check the correct answer.*)

______ *a.* the conclusion is wrong
______ *b.* the paragraphs don't relate to the same topic
______ *c.* the last two paragraphs are in the wrong order

c

583

Looking at the last two topic sentences in the previous frame, what would you have to do to correct your paragraph order?

______ *a.* *Reverse* the order of the last two paragraphs.
______ *b.* *Drop* the last paragraph.

Answer ____________
(*a*) or (*b*)

a

(You still need the paragraph beginning "Also, today there are only a few places in which fish can survive," since it is *evidence* to support your conclusion.)

584

When you find something in your writing that needs correcting, you should *mark it* on the paper. That way you won't forget to correct it when you rewrite.

For example, here's how to *mark* an out-of-order paragraph.

> ^From these two observations, it seems obvious that water pollution has greatly increased in our country. . . . If it is, we can only *conclude* that we will someday be faced with a crisis in our water supply.
>
> [Also, today there are only a few . . . in the nearby streams.]

What do these marks indicate you should do when you rewrite?

____

____

(*Your own words*)

Change the order of the paragraphs, put the last paragraph before the next-to-last, and so on.

585

The brackets ([. . .]) at each end of the paragraph show that the *whole paragraph* should be moved, not just a sentence or a word.

The ^ mark shows *where* the paragraph in brackets should be moved. The line connecting the [and the ^ shows movement.

Mark the following paragraphs so that you know the second paragraph should come before the first.

> A few of these signs are rising employment, rising educational levels, and the increasing number of agencies providing emergency help. These tendencies lead to hope that the rising rate of poverty can be held down.
>
> Statistics since 1960 show that the amount of poverty in the county is increasing. In 1960, 11 percent of the population fell below the poverty line. In 1966, the figure was 14 percent. Still, there are signs now that this trend to increasing poverty may be slowing down.

A few of these signs are rising employment, rising educational levels, and the increasing number of agencies providing emergency help. These tendencies lead to hope that the rising rate of poverty can be held down.

[Statistics since 1960 show that the amount of poverty in the county is increasing. In 1960, 11 percent of the population fell below the poverty line. In 1966, the figure was 14 percent. Still, there are signs now that this trend to increasing poverty may be slowing down.]

or

[A few of these signs are rising employment, rising educational levels, and the increasing number of agencies providing emergency help. These tendencies lead to hope that the rising rate of poverty can be held down.]

Statistics since 1960 show that the amount of poverty in the county is increasing. In 1960, 11 percent of the population fell below the poverty line. In 1966, the figure was 14 percent. Still, there are signs now that this trend to increasing poverty may be slowing down.

586

Read through the following paragraphs. Decide whether they are in the right order. Then mark the paragraphs so that you know their order should be reversed.

> The study showed that first-grade children from crowded, noisy environments could not tell their teacher's voice from the sound of a truck outside. They could only hear a few words of any sentence spoken to them. These discoveries made clear several of the physical reasons why the children had trouble adjusting to school.
>
> It often happens that children from very noisy, crowded environments have trouble when they start school. Many teachers have wondered why certain children have a hard time from the very beginning. A study was performed in one city to examine these questions as they affected a group of first graders.

The study showed that first-grade children from crowded, noisy environments could not tell their teacher's voice from the sound of a truck outside. They could only hear a few words of any sentence spoken to them. These discoveries made clear several of the physical reasons why the children had trouble adjusting to school.

[It often happens that children from very noisy, crowded environments have trouble when they start school. Many teachers have wondered why certain children have a hard time from the very beginning. A study was performed in one city to examine these questions as they affected a group of first graders.]

or

[The study showed that first-grade children from crowded, noisy environments could not tell their teacher's voice from the sound of a truck outside. They could only hear a few words of any sentence spoken to them. These discoveries made clear several of the physical reasons why the children had trouble adjusting to school.]

It often happens that children from very noisy, crowded environments have trouble when they start school. Many teachers have wondered why certain children have a hard time from the very beginning. A study was performed in one city to examine these questions as they affected a group of first graders.

587

Now suppose you found that the topic sentences you underlined were:

1. To find out the facts about water pollution look around at the area in which you live.
2. For instance, now there are signs at the creeks warning people that swimming in them is dangerous.
3. It's true that the creeks are not safe to swim in.
4. Also, today there are only a few places in which fish can still survive.
5. From these two observations, it seems obvious that water pollution has greatly increased in our county.

You can see that: (*Check the correct answer.*)

______ *a.* Paragraphs 3 and 4 should be reversed.
______ *b.* Paragraphs 2 and 3 repeat the same information.
______ *c.* Paragraph 1 isn't necessary.

b

588
If two paragraphs give approximately the same information, you are more likely to improve your paper by:

a. *Dropping* one of the paragraphs
b. *Reversing* their order

Answer ____________
(*a*) or (*b*)

a

The purpose of a paragraph is to give information. If a paragraph repeats what has already been said, it is probably unnecessary and should be crossed out.

589
1. If you find that a paragraph is out of order:
   a. when you reread, you should ______________________________
   b. when you rewrite, you should ______________________________
2. If you find that a paragraph doesn't support the main purpose of the paper, you should ______________________________

1. *a.* mark it
   b. move it
2. drop it (cross it out)

590
We have been talking about correcting your writing in steps. Let's review the first step—namely, reading your paper for sense only, in order to check on overall clarity and organization.

Read the following paragraphs. *Underline* the first sentences, and read them carefully. Then *mark* the paragraphs so that you will know what to correct.

1. In 1876, a librarian named Melvil Dewey invented the Dewey system of classifying knowledge. This system divided books into categories according to their subject. These categories represented different "types" of knowledge.

2. For example, the first group of books is the group which contains encyclopedias and dictionaries. The books in this group do not have any one "subject" and are a source for general information.

3. These are only two of the ten main groups. Each of these groups is then divided into smaller groups. There are about 100 groups in all, which makes it possible to classify easily almost any book on any subject.

4. The second group of books is the group that deals with philosophy. Under this heading come the books concerning general questions about man's life and writings by famous philosophers like Plato and Aristotle.

5. The many large and small groups together apply to almost any book. This is an easy way to classify books.

---

1. In 1876, a librarian named Melvil Dewey invented the Dewey system of classifying knowledge. This system divided books into categories according to their subject. These categories represented different "types" of knowledge.

2. For example, the first group of books is the group which contains encyclopedias and dictionaries. The books in this group do not have any one "subject" and are a source for general information.

3. These are only two of the ten main groups. Each of these groups is then divided into smaller groups. There are about 100 groups in all, which makes it possible to classify easily almost any book on any subject.

4. [The second group of books is the group that deals with philosophy. Under this heading come the books concerning general questions about man's life and writings by famous philosophers like Plato and Aristotle]

~~5. The many large and small groups together apply to almost any book. This is an easy way to classify books.~~

(You should have crossed out paragraph 5, because it gives the *same* information as paragraph 3. Therefore, it isn't necessary.)

Once you have checked the overall organization of your paper and made the necessary markings, you are ready for the second step in the revising process.

591

The second step is to go back and check the organization of *each individual paragraph.*

You should check *each paragraph* for the three points we emphasized earlier:

1. time order
2. development of one idea
3. variety of sentence structure

Go to the next frame

no answer required

592

Suppose you are rereading this paragraph, in which the *time order* is incorrect.

1. In 1876, the Dewey classification system was invented. 2. Now it is used all over the country. 3. It has been revised several times since then, but the basic groups have remained the same.

Which sentences should exchange places? (*Check the correct answer.*)

_____ *a.* 1 and 3
_____ *b.* 1 and 2
_____ *c.* 2 and 3

c

Sentences 2 and 3 should change places, because sentence 3 refers to something that happened *before* sentence 2.

593

When you discover incorrect *time order* in a paragraph, you should *mark* it so that you will remember to correct the paragraph when you rewrite.

Here are two ways of doing this.

In 1876, the Dewey classification system was invented. [Now it is used all over the country.] It has been revised several times since then, but the basic groups have remained the same.

In 1876, the Dewey classification system was invented. Now it is used all over the country. [It has been revised several times since then, but the basic groups have remained the same.]

In both these examples, the brackets ([. . .]) show what is to be moved, the mark shows *where* the material should be moved to, and the line between indicates movement.

When you *rewrite* your paper and see these marks, you will know that you should ______________________________

____

(*Your own words*)

move the sentence in brackets to where the ^ mark is

594

The following paragraph contains sentences that are out of order. *Mark* it so that you will know what to correct.

> When I first traveled on a plane, I was terrified. Now I feel much more secure. Since then, I flew two more times and nothing happened.

Your marking should look like one of these:

When I first traveled on a plane, I was terrified. [Now I feel much more secure.] Since then, I flew two more times and nothing happened. ^

When I first traveled on a plane, I was terrified. ^ Now I feel much more secure. [Since then, I flew two more times and nothing happened.]

595

We said earlier that all sentences in a paragraph should relate to the idea being developed. If you find a paragraph with a sentence that doesn't belong, *cross it out*.

In the following paragraph, cross out the sentence that doesn't belong.

> Auto racing is a dangerous sport. Every year several drivers, mechanics, and spectators are killed. Safety precautions are very limited when such high speeds are involved. Soccer is dangerous, too.

Auto racing is a dangerous sport. Every year several drivers, mechanics, and spectators are killed. Safety precautions are very limited when such high speeds are involved. ~~Soccer is dangerous, too.~~

596

In the following paragraph, decide whether the last sentence should be *dropped* or *moved.* If it should be dropped, cross it out. If it should be moved, mark it so that it is clear where it should be moved in the paragraph.

> The leaders of the women's suffrage movement were an unusual group. This is indicated by the fact that more than 60 percent of these women had been to college. One mark of their difference, then, was their level of education. This fact is unusual because at the beginning of the twentieth century, when these women were campaigning, less than 5 percent of the general female population went to college.

The leaders of the women's suffrage movement were an unusual group. This is indicated by the fact that more than 60 percent of these women had been to college. One mark of their difference, then, was their level of education. [This fact is unusual because at the beginning of the twentieth century, when these women were campaigning, less than 5 percent of the general female population went to college.]

597

Another point about a good paragraph is that the sentences should vary as to type. If you find a paragraph that sounds dull because the same sentence type is used throughout, you should *mark it* so that you will remember to change it when you rewrite.

Suppose you see a paragraph that begins with three simple sentences in a row:

> The night was cold. The wind howled. The tree limbs shook.

Here's how to make the last two *simple* sentences into a compound sentence:

> The night was cold. The wind howled, and the tree limbs shook.

The marks above tell you to make three *changes* when you rewrite.

1. Change the period to a ______________ .
2. Between "howled" and "The," insert the word ______________ .
3. Change the capital *T* in "The" to a ______________ .

1. comma
2. and
3. small *t*

598

The marks used in the example in the previous frame act as reminders to change the two simple sentences to one compound sentence during rewriting.

Show how you would *mark* the sentences below to make one compound sentence. Remember all three steps in the previous frame.

The fuse blew. The lights went out.

The fuse blew, and the lights went out.

599

Mark the following paragraphs so that you will remember to combine the second and third sentences.

The child's mother was frantic. She had left her baby in the stroller. She had gone into the store. When she came back, the baby was gone.

The child's mother was frantic. She had left her baby in the stroller, and she had gone into the store. When she came back, the baby was gone.

600

Now read the following paragraph:

There are only a few old houses left on our street. The new offices were built. All the old buildings were torn down. New houses are fine, but I wish some of the old homes had been preserved.

Mark the second and third sentences above to indicate a complex sentence by:

1. inserting "When" before "The"
2. changing the *T* in "The" to a small *t*
3. changing the period after "built" to a comma
4. changing the *A* in "All" to a small *a*

There are only a few old houses left on our street. When the new offices were built, all the old buildings were torn down. New houses are fine, but I wish some of the old homes had been preserved.

601

The four changes you marked in the previous frame would change the two *simple* sentences to one ______________ sentence.

(compound) (complex)

complex

602

Now read the following paragraph:

> The state park is the best place to picnic. The picnic grounds are huge, and there is a pool nearby. There are also ten miles of trails, and a hike along them leads you to the famous waterfall.

In our opinion, this paragraph could be improved by changing the third sentence (which is compound) into two simple ones. Here's how to mark it:

> There are also ten miles of trails, ~~and~~ a hike along them leads you to the famous waterfall.

We made three changes in these sentences.

1. s⊙ means "Change the comma into a ______________ ."
2. ~~and~~ means "Take out the word ______________ ."
3. a means "Change the small *a* to a ______________ ."

1. period
2. and
3. capital *A*

603

A good way to check for subject and verb agreement is to go through each of your sentences and pick out the subject and verb. This may show you an agreement mistake that you missed when you first wrote the sentence.

Read the following paragraph. Look for the subject and verb in each sentence. If you find a verb that doesn't agree with its subject, *cross it out* and insert the correct form of the verb like this: "It ~~don't~~ doesn't matter whether or not I rewrite this."

> Rewriting papers seem like a waste of time to me. It's hard enough for me to write a paper once. Besides, each of my teachers have said he can't read my handwriting, so I shouldn't have to read it either.

Rewriting papers ~~seem~~ seems like a waste of time to me. It's hard enough for me to write a paper once. Besides, each of my teachers ~~have~~ has said he can't read my handwriting, so I shouldn't have to read it either.

604

While you are checking the verbs in your paragraphs, check to see if you have changed tenses in the middle of a paragraph. People often forget what tense they are using, especially when they are writing a story.

Read the following paragraph. Find the sentence where the verb tense shifts and correct the rest of the verbs in the paragraph the same way you corrected the verbs in the previous frame.

> The detective reached carefully to turn on the light. Suddenly, from the other side of the dark room, he heard a noise. He falls to the floor, rolls beneath a table, and shines his flashlight toward the sound. It's only a cat.

The detective reached carefully to turn on the light. Suddenly, from the other side of the dark room, he heard a noise. He ~~falls~~ fell to the floor, ~~rolls~~ rolled beneath a table, and ~~shines~~ shone his flashlight toward the sound. It~~'s~~ was only a cat.

Rewrite the paragraph in the space below, making the changes indicated by your correction marks.

The detective reached carefully to turn on the light. Suddenly, from the other side of the dark room, he heard a noise. He fell to the floor, rolled beneath a table, and shone his flashlight toward the sound. It was only a cat.

605

Also, check your use of *plurals.* If there is a noun whose plural you are not sure of, look it up in a dictionary.

Read the paragraph below and see if the plurals are correct. Cross out the incorrect forms and insert the correct ones.

> When we arrived in Canada, the leafs were just beginning to turn brown. A short time later the first snow fell, and we bought skiies. By the time we had been there six months, we were fairly good skier.

When we arrived in Canada, the ~~leafs~~ leaves were just beginning to turn brown. A short time later the first snow fell, and we bought ~~skiies~~ skis. By the time we had been there six months, we were fairly good skiers.

606

Also, check your *pronouns* to be sure they are in correct form. Decide whether each pronoun you use is a *subject* or an *object*, and use the correct form for each.

Read the paragraph below, and check each pronoun. If it is in the wrong form, cross it out and insert the correct form.

> The agreement was made secretly between Mr. Wilson and he. When the rest of the group heard about it, they decided to hold a special election to put both men out of office. My brother and me were the only ones who objected, so the election was held.

The agreement was made secretly between Mr. Wilson and ~~he~~ him. When the rest of the group heard about it, they decided to hold a special election to put both men out of office. My brother and ~~me~~ I were the only ones who objected, so the election was held.

607

In the following sentences, cross out or change the commas which have been used incorrectly.

1. I sent her a present, she sent me a card.
2. Steve drove through a stop sign, and a red light.
3. That house was for sale, it was sold yesterday.

1. I sent her a present. She sent me a card.
2. Steve drove through a stop sign and a red light.
3. That house was for sale. It was sold yesterday.

608

In the following sentences, insert commas where they are needed.

1. As soon as the sun came up we left.
2. The car stopped stalled and flooded.
3. Our aunt the teacher is staying with us.

1. As soon as the sun came up, we left.
2. The car stopped, stalled, and flooded.
3. Our aunt, the teacher, is staying with us.

One of the most important things to check before you rewrite your final draft is your use of *commas.* If you have used commas where they don't belong, cross them out. If you have *not* used them where they are needed, insert them.

609

Read the following paragraph and check each sentence to see if you have used commas correctly. *Cross out* unnecessary commas and insert missing ones.

> When the rains finally stopped it was too late, to repair the damage. Thousands of homes, farm barns and fields, had been flooded. Crops were destroyed by the acre and herds of wild animals died. It was the worst flood, that the area had ever experienced.

When the rains finally stopped, it was too late to repair the damage. Thousands of homes, farm barns, and fields had been flooded. Crops were destroyed by the acre, and herds of wild animals died. It was the worst flood that the area had ever experienced.

610

You should also check over your papers for *capitalization* mistakes: not only beginnings of sentences, but names and proper adjectives, too.

Mark the following paragraph wherever there is a mistake in capitalization.

> Suddenly we heard a voice over the intercom. It was the plane's Pilot, telling us that the weather was worse and that we would have to land at Gander, newfoundland. We were there for two days, and i've never seen such a barren place. Ice stretched as far as you could see. When we finally got home on sunday, the sunshine was the most welcome thing I'd seen in Days.

Suddenly we heard a voice over the intercom. It was the plane's Pilot, telling us that the weather was worse and that we would have to land at Gander, newfoundland. We were there for two days, and i've never seen such a barren place. Ice stretched as far as you could see. When we finally got home on sunday, the sunshine was the most welcome thing I'd seen in Days.

611

We have reviewed several basic grammar details to check in rereading what you have written: agreement, verb tenses, pronoun forms, plurals, punctuation, and capitalization.

It is best to look for these details: (*Check the correct answer.*)

______ *a.* before you check overall organization
______ *b.* before you check individual paragraph structure
______ *c.* after you have checked overall organization and individual paragraph structure

c

612

In your own words, what are the three main steps in checking over what you have written—prior to a rewrite of the final draft copy.

1. ______
2. ______
3. ______

(*Your own words*)

1. check *overall* organization
2. check individual *paragraph* structure
3. check for grammar details

613

Suppose you have decided that the following paragraphs are organized clearly and that their individual structure is good. Now read them over carefully and *check* for grammar details. *Mark* errors in agreement, tense, pronouns, plurals, punctuation, and capitalization.

Edward r. Murrow a wartime reporter has said that the atmosphere during the bombing of London reminded him of a ghost town in nevada. The antiaircraft guns swept hot wind across the Streets and carried dust everywhere.

The streets are not only blazing hot and dusty, but they are also deserted. There is no people and no Taxies. Everyone are carrying their mattress and food into "safe" office buildings.

When the bombing and shooting stopped, people cautiously began appearing on the streets again. However, by Nightfall the sirens would always begin and total emptiness returned to the streets.

Edward r. Murrow a wartime reporter has said that the atmosphere during the bombing of London reminded him of a ghost town in nevada. The antiaircraft guns swept hot wind across the Streets and carried dust everywhere.

The streets are not only blazing hot and dusty, but they are also deserted. There is no people and no Taxies. Everyone are carrying their mattress and food into "safe" office buildings.

When the bombing and shooting stopped, people cautiously began appearing on the streets again. However, by Nightfall the sirens would always begin and total emptiness returned to the streets.

614

Below are two paragraphs which should be revised. Read them through *once,* checking first for overall organization. *Then mark the paragraphs if they are out of order.*

The boat ride was five hour long. We traveled all the way to the end of the lake and back. a distance of sixty-four mile. along the way we pass among green islands, and tall mountains. When the trip ended I decided that it had been the more peaceful and beautiful ride I have ever took.

When we first arrive at the lake I didnt know what to do. Finally my friend said, let's go on the boat ride. There seem to be so many things happening that I couldn't make up, my mind. I said, "All right," and we got on the boat.

The boat ride was five hour long. We traveled all the way to the end of the lake and back. a distance of sixty-four mile. along the way we pass among green islands, and tall mountains. When the trip ended I decided that it had been the more peaceful and beautiful ride I have ever took.

When we first arrive at the lake I didnt know what to do. Finally my friend said, let's go on the boat ride. There seem to be so many things happening that I couldn't make up, my mind. I said, "All right," and we got on the boat.

615

Now reread the paragraphs again. This time check to see how well *each paragraph* is organized. If you find a sentence that is out of order, *mark it* so that you will know where to place it when you rewrite.

The boat ride was five hour long. We traveled all the way to the end of the lake and back. a distance of sixty-four mile. along the way we pass among green islands, and tall mountains. When the trip ended I decided that it had been the more peaceful and beautiful ride I have ever took.

When we first arrive at the lake I didnt know what to do. Finally my friend said, let's go on the boat ride. There seem to be so many things happening that I couldn't make up, my mind. I said, "All right," and we got on the boat.

The boat ride was five hour long. We traveled all the way to the end of the lake and back. a distance of sixty-four mile. along the way we pass among green islands, and tall mountains. When the trip ended I decided that it had been the more peaceful and beautiful ride I have ever took.

[When we first arrive at the lake I didnt know what to do. Finally my friend said, let's go on the boat ride. [There seem to be so many things happening that I couldn't make up, my mind.] I said, "All right," and we got on the boat.]

616

Now, reread the paragraph a *third* time. Check for grammar mistakes and *mark each one* that you find so that you will know how to correct it when you rewrite.

The boat ride was five hour long. We traveled all the way to the end of the lake and back. a distance of sixty-four mile. along the way we pass among green islands, and tall mountains. When the trip ended I decided that it had been the more peaceful and beautiful ride I have ever took.

When we first arrive at the lake I didnt know what to do. Finally my friend said, let's go on the boat ride. There seem to be so many things happening that I couldn't make up, my mind. I said, "All right," and we got on the boat.

The boat ride was five hour long. We traveled all the way to the end of the lake and back. a distance of sixty-four mile. along the way we pass among green islands, and tall mountains. When the trip ended I decided that it had been the more peaceful and beautiful ride I have ever took.

When we first arrive at the lake I didnt know what to do. Finally my friend said, let's go on the boat ride. There seem to be so many things happening that I couldn't make up, my mind. I said, "All right," and we got on the boat.

617

Now *rewrite the paragraphs* making all the corrections indicated in your answer.

The boat ride was five hour long. We traveled all the way to the end of the lake and back. a distance of sixty-four mile. along the way we pass among green islands, and tall mountains. When the trip ended I decided that it had been the more peaceful and beautiful ride I have ever took.

When we first arrive at the lake I didnt know what to do. Finally my friend said, let's go on the boat ride. There seem to be so many things happening that I couldn't make up, my mind. I said, "All right," and we got on the boat.

When we first arrived at the lake, I didn't know what to do. There seemed to be so many things happening that I couldn't make up my mind. Finally my friend said, "Let's go on the boat ride." I said, "All right," and we got on the boat.

The boat ride was five hours long. We traveled all the way to the end of the lake and back, a distance of sixty-four miles. Along the way we passed among green islands and tall mountains. When the trip ended, I decided that it had been the most peaceful and beautiful ride I have ever taken.

618

Below are several paragraphs which should be revised. Read them through *once,* checking first for overall organization. Then *mark the paragraphs which are out of order* so that they can be rewritten correctly.

Until now, most of the earths weather have been completely unnoticed. Because, large areas of the ocean and some land areas do not have, weather stations. this has made it difficult to forecast weather in other parts of the world.

once these computers and satellites are developed more than forecasting can be done, with the weather. In fact it may eventually be possible to change earths climate to suit the weather expert's.

With these satellites and computers to cover the unknown weather areas a worldwide weather forecast would be possible, these forecasts could be accurate as much as two week's in advance. The United States is presently testing new weather satellites and orbiting computers.

Until now, most of the earths weather have been completely unnoticed. Because, large areas of the ocean and some land areas do not have, weather stations. this has made it difficult to forecast weather in other parts of the world.

once these computers and satellites are developed more than forecasting can be done, with the weather. In fact it may eventually be possible to change earths climate to suit the weather expert's.

[With these satellites and computers to cover the unknown weather areas a worldwide weather forecast would be possible, these forecasts could be accurate as much as two week's in advance. The United States is presently testing new weather satellites and orbiting computers.]

619

Now read the paragraphs through again, this time checking each individual paragraph for organization and sentence structure. Mark the sentences below which are out of order so that they can be rewritten correctly.

Until now, most of the earths weather have been completely unnoticed. Because, large areas of the ocean and some land areas do not have, weather stations. this has made it difficult to forecast weather in other parts of the world.

once these computers and satellites are developed more than forecasting can be done, with the weather. In fact it may eventually be possible to change earths climate to suit the weather expert's.

[With these satellites and computers to cover the unknown weather areas a worldwide weather forecast would be possible, these forecasts could be accurate as much as two week's in advance. The United States is presently testing new weather satellites and orbiting computers.]

Until now, most of the earths weather have been completely unnoticed. Because, large areas of the ocean and some land areas do not have, weather stations. this has made it difficult to forecast weather in other parts of the world.

once these computers and satellites are developed more than forecasting can be done, with the weather. In fact it may eventually be possible to change earths climate to suit the weather expert's.

With these satellites and computers to cover the unknown weather areas a worldwide weather forecast would be possible, these forecasts could be accurate as much as two week's in advance. The United States is presently testing new weather satellites and orbiting computers.

620

Now, read the paragraphs a third time. *Mark all the grammatical details which should be corrected* (commas, capital letters, etc.).

Until now, most of the earths weather have been completely unnoticed. Because, large areas of the ocean and some land areas do not have, weather stations. this has made it difficult to forecast weather in other parts of the world.

once these computers and satellites are developed more than forecasting can be done, with the weather. In fact it may eventually be possible to change earths climate to suit the weather expert's.

With these satellites and computers to cover the unknown weather areas a worldwide weather forecast would be possible, these forecasts could be accurate as much as two week's in advance. The United States is presently testing new weather satellites and orbiting computers.

Until now, most of the earths weather have been completely unnoticed. Because, large areas of the ocean and some land areas do not have, weather stations. this has made it difficult to forecast weather in other parts of the world.

once these computers and satellites are developed more than forecasting can be done, with the weather. In fact it may eventually be possible to change earths climate to suit the weather expert's.

With these satellites and computers to cover the unknown weather areas a worldwide weather forecast would be possible, these forecasts could be accurate as much as two week's in advance. The United States is presently testing new weather satellites and orbiting computers.

621

Now *rewrite* the three paragraphs, using your markings as a guide.

Until now, most of the earths weather have been completely unnoticed. Because large areas of the ocean and some land areas do not have weather stations. this has made it difficult to forecast weather in other parts of the world.

once these computers and satellites are developed more than forecasting can be done with the weather. In fact it may eventually be possible to change earths climate to suit the weather expert's.

With these satellites and computers to cover the unknown weather areas a worldwide weather forecast would be possible these forecasts could be accurate as much as two week's in advance. The United States is presently testing new weather satellites and orbiting computers.

Until now, most of the earth's weather has been completely unnoticed, because large areas of the ocean and some land areas do not have weather stations. This has made it difficult to forecast weather in other parts of the world.

The United States is presently testing new weather satellites and orbiting computers. With these satellites and computers to cover the unknown weather areas, a worldwide weather forecast would be possible. These forecasts could be accurate as much as two weeks in advance.

Once these computers and satellites are developed, more than forecasting can be done with the weather. In fact, it may eventually be possible to change earth's climate to suit the weather experts.

622

Now read and reread the following paragraphs, using all three checking steps and *marking* where corrections are necessary.

The plate that is used to produce Photographs are called the *negative*. On the negative, the light and dark areas of the finished photograph are reversed. Two steps are involved in preparing a Negative before a photograph can be produced.

The first step is called *developing*. It is performed in a darkroom. No light at all should strike the negative. Until the second step is performed any light will destroy the image.

Production, of the finished picture is called *printing*, this is done by putting the negative between a light, and a special kind of Paper. This reverses the light and dark areas again and produces a finished Photograph.

The second step which protects the negative from light is called *fixing*. fixing is done by placing the developed film into a liquid chemical, then it is ready for production.

The plate that is used to produce Photographs are called the *negative.* On the negative, the light and dark areas of the finished photograph are reversed. Two steps are involved in preparing a Negative before a photograph can be produced.

The first step is called *developing.* It is performed in a darkroom; No light at all should strike the negative. Until the second step is performed any light will destroy the image.

Production, of the finished picture is called *printing* this is done by putting the negative between a light, and a special kind of Paper. This reverses the light and dark areas again and produces a finished Photograph.

[The second step which protects the negative from light is called *fixing.* fixing is done by placing the developed film into a liquid chemical then it is ready for production.]

623

Rewrite the four paragraphs in the previous frame, making all the corrections indicated.

The plate that is used to produce photographs is called the *negative.* On the negative, the light and dark areas of the finished photograph are reversed. Two steps are involved in preparing a negative before a photograph can be produced.

The first step is called *developing.* It is performed in a darkroom, and no light at all should strike the negative. Until the second step is performed, any light will destroy the image.

The second step, which protects the negative from light, is called *fixing.* Fixing is done by placing the developed film into a liquid chemical. Then it is ready for production.

Production of the finished picture is called *printing.* This is done by putting the negative between a light and a special kind of paper. This reverses the light and dark areas again and produces a finished photograph.

624

Read through the following paragraphs, using each of the three checking steps. Indicate where corrections should be made.

Jules Verne a frenchman wrote an account of a voyage to the moon more than, one hundred years ago, although his story was imaginary much of it is surprisingly similar to twentieth-century flights.

Verne sent up three astronauts as in the apollo program. They blasted off from Florida not far from Cape kennedy, and found the moon's surface "dreary, inhospitable, unearthly." Finally he also chose the ocean as the best "splashdown" location.

All these coincidences indicate, that science fiction can become scientific fact. Verne described an elaborate system, to keep his astronauts alive in space just as scientist's today have done for ours. He also gave them the same pride in discovery that our modern explorer's possess.

Jules Verne a frenchman wrote an account of a voyage to the moon more than one hundred years ago although his story was imaginary much of it is surprisingly similar to twentieth-century flights.

Verne sent up three astronauts as in the apollo program. They blasted off from Florida not far from Cape kennedy, and found the moon's surface "dreary, inhospitable, unearthly." Finally he also chose the ocean as the best "splashdown" location.

[All these coincidences indicate, that science fiction can become scientific fact.] Verne described an elaborate system, to keep his astronauts alive in space just as scientist's today have done for ours. He also gave them the same pride in discovery that our modern explorer's possess.

625

Using the marks in your answer to frame 624 as a guide, rewrite the paragraphs.

Jules Verne, a Frenchman, wrote an account of a voyage to the moon more than one hundred years ago. Although his story was imaginary, much of it is surprisingly similar to twentieth-century flights.

Verne sent up three astronauts as in the Apollo program. They blasted off from Florida not far from Cape Kennedy and found the moon's surface "dreary, inhospitable, unearthly." Finally he also chose the ocean as the best "splashdown" location.

Verne described an elaborate system to keep his astronauts alive in space just as scientists today have done for ours. He also gave them the same pride in discovery that our modern explorers possess. All these coincidences indicate that science fiction can become scientific fact.

626

The report is due tomorrow for my 10:00 A.M. class and here it is 2:00 in the morning and I'm just getting started! What was it that the teacher stressed about writing? Oh yes, there are four steps to follow in writing any "good" paper: (1) write—to get the ideas on paper, (2) rewrite—to make sure the message is clear and reads as intended, (3) edit—to be sure that the punctuation and grammar are correct, and (4) proofread—to check for any typographical errors.

At this moment, I think "Panic" would be a great topic for this paper. I'm not even certain that the paper is at the "write" stage!

I think I need some form of extra stimulation to get my act together. What will it be . . . strong drink of some kind to whet my imagination, or a hot, caffeine-loaded cup of coffee or tea to make me alert? . . . Or is it a matter of fatigue and lack of inspirational readiness? I think I'll catch about four hours sleep and try again when I'm less tired. . . .

This selection is intended to be correct as written. If you rewrite parts of it, you are exercising your personal stylistic preferences. Developing a style that is grammatically appropriate and also delivers your message clearly to your reader is the key to writing power. It is hoped that by now you feel comfortable, knowledgeable, and confident that you can write at this level. Remember, the best way to develop your writing power is to *write often*!

627

This book ends as it began, with a diagnosis of your writing skill. Before writing your sample, let's review the steps you've learned about writing good paragraphs. First, identify a topic you'd like to write about. Second, brainstorm and list all the ideas you have on the topic. Third, organize your ideas in outline form so that you have a reasonable sequence in mind. Fourth, begin writing, trying to use your outline as the base for your paragraph. Fifth, read what you have written to see that your intended meaning is clear; rewrite what is not. Sixth, edit what you've written for grammar and punctuation precision. Seventh, proofread your paper as a check against accidental mistakes.

Your instructor will check your progress on this "final" sample. You should be ready to be on your own in college writing now; good luck!

____

____

____

____

____

____

____

____

____

____

____

____

____

____